PRAISE FOR
QUICK & EASY PALEO COMFORT FOODS

"[The Mayfields'] passion and experience come through in their writing...and the amazing quality of their meals. A fantastic cookbook."

—From the foreword by Robb Wolf, *New York Times* bestselling author of *The Paleo Solution*

"What a perfect follow-up to their bestselling cookbook, *Paleo Comfort Foods*. This is the perfect cookbook for those who are in a hurry and need something tasty and simple. Bravo to the Mayfields."

—Mark Sisson, bestselling author of *The Primal Blueprint* and publisher of Mark's Daily Apple

"I find cookbooks fascinating, as they are a glimpse into the people and cultures that created them. Charles and Julie are very talented and their creations have quickly become staples in the Welbourn household. I consider their book a must-have for Paleo/ Primal eaters."

—John Welbourn, NFL veteran, founder of CrossFit Football, creator of Power Athlete and one of the founding members of Well Food Company

"The 'I don't have time to cook!' excuse is no longer valid. If you're a busy parent sprinting between soccer practice and the dinner table, or a bachelor entrepreneur like me, you can't manufacture time. So your best bet is putting this book in your arsenal!"

—Kyle Maynard, two-time ESPY award winning athlete and author of the *New York Times* bestseller *No Excuses*

"It's generally assumed that eating healthy and eating well, as far as taste goes, are mutually exclusive. Charles and Julie turn that idea on its head and prove that you can eat great-tasting food that's great for you. Combine that with the fact that these recipes are all relatively quick and easy, and you've got a go-to resource for any cook. Eating Paleo has made a huge difference for me. Healthy, tasty and convenient: what more can you ask for?"

—Chris Hall, Executive Chef, Local Three

QUICK & EASY
PALEO
COMFORT FOODS

QUICK & EASY
PALEO
COMFORT FOODS

100+ DELICIOUS GLUTEN-FREE RECIPES

Julie and Charles Mayfield

Foreword by *New York Times* bestselling author Robb Wolf

Photography by Mark Adams

QUICK & EASY PALEO COMFORT FOODS
ISBN-13: 978-0373-89280-8

© 2013 by Julie and Charles Mayfield

All photography © Mark Adams, except pages xiii, 10 (iStockphoto), 77 (Photodisc/Getty Images), 126, 127 (iStockphoto), 230 (Photodisc/Getty Images), 231, 232 (iStockphoto).

The health advice presented in this book is intended only as an informative resource guide to help you make informed decisions; it is not meant to replace the advice of a physician or to serve as a guide to self-treatment. Always seek competent medical help for any health condition or if there is any question about the appropriateness of a procedure or health recommendation.

Library of Congress Cataloging-in-Publication Data

Mayfield, Julie.
Quick & easy paleo comfort foods : 150 delicious gluten-free recipes / Julie and Charles Mayfield ; foreword by *New York Times* bestselling author Robb Wolf ; photography by Mark Adams.
   pages cm
  Includes index.
   ISBN 978-0-373-89280-8 (pbk.)
1. Gluten-free diet--Recipes. 2. Gluten-free foods. 3. Prehistoric peoples--Food. 4. Quick and easy cooking. I. Mayfield, Charles. II. Title. III. Title: Quick and easy paleo comfort foods.
  RM237.86.M372 2013
  641.5'55--dc23

2013024005

www.Harlequin.com

Printed in U.S.A.

For Charles Scott Mayfield IV.
You are our sunshine.
And in memory of Buzz.

CONTENTS

Foreword x

Introduction xiii

CHAPTER 1
Our Paleo Definition 1

CHAPTER 2
Starters and Snacks 14

CHAPTER 3
Soups, Stews and Salads 40

CHAPTER 4
Main Dishes 74

CHAPTER 5
Sides and Sauces 164

CHAPTER 6
Sweets and Treats 222

Converting to Metrics 242

Acknowledgments 243

Index 246

FOREWORD

Unless you have been living under a rock (or perhaps in a cave) you have likely heard of this "Paleo" diet concept. Heck, you are actually HOLDING a book about Paleo cooking right now! I started investigating this way of eating and living nearly fifteen years ago as a biochemist interested in autoimmunity and cancer research. I had a particularly focused attention on this topic as I was unfortunately the victim of a mismatch between my old-school genetics and our modern food supply. I had high blood pressure, terrible blood lipids and ulcerative colitis so bad my doctors wanted to perform a bowel resection.

I was the ripe old age of twenty-eight.

To say that Paleo saved my life is honestly an understatement and does not really paint the big picture beyond my health problems and what types of food I eat. The Paleo concept has transformed my world by not only returning me to health, but by putting me in contact with people who have become lifelong friends. This book, written by Charles and Julie Mayfield, is yet another example of the many ways this way of eating has improved my life. I met Charles and Jules many years ago after giving a seminar in Florida. We all went out to eat together and had a great time hanging out. How was I to know that this simple meeting over good food would grow into my good friends writing the type of cookbooks I'd love to write … if I were that good in the kitchen? Let me relate a short story about all that:

I was in Atlanta for the release of my first book, *The Paleo Solution*. I had just made the *New York Times* bestseller list, things were going great, and as publishers are wont to do, mine was pestering me about doing a cookbook to complement my main book. I'm pretty handy in the kitchen, but my skills are not up to the task of doing a really solid cookbook. The usual thing that happens after writing a successful diet book is you go looking for a registered dietician/chef to do 99 percent of the heavy lifting of recipe generation and writing, then you slap your *New York Times* bestselling name on the cover and you now have your second book rolling. I was heading down this path until Julie handed me a cup of her Country Curry (over cauliflower "rice"). With the first bite I realized I could not do what most authors do. I'd be a fraud. The book I'd want to do was sitting in the heads of the two kitchen-geeks watching me devour bowl after bowl of Thai hot curry. Between spoonfuls I told Charles and Jules they needed to do a book. They did and it crushed. The books THEY write are the books I WISH I could write. Where their first book, *Paleo Comfort Foods,* was the epitome of gourmet eating, *Quick & Easy Paleo Comfort Foods* maintains all the high standards and taste of the first book, but with an eye towards time efficiency and ease of preparation. If I have heard one comment over the years it is that people need help, not only in eating healthy, but also in how to prep meals quickly. With *Quick & Easy Paleo Comfort Foods,* everything you need to fuel yourself and your family is covered.

So, is this a good cookbook? Yes, it's fantastic. The reason why is good things come from passion. Passion for a topic is a bit like dancing: impossible to fake. Charles and Julie are immersed in a lifestyle that involves running a gym, tinkering in the kitchen and being deeply involved in their local sustainable food scene. That passion and experience come through in their writing, their attention to detail and, most importantly for you, in the amazing quality of their meals. I love this book because it is the book I'd write if I were as good at this stuff as Charles and Jules are. So please consider this not only a fantastic cookbook—which happens to focus on Paleo foods—but consider this the quasi-official cookbook for *The Paleo Solution.*

Robb Wolf, *New York Times* **bestselling author of** *The Paleo Solution*

INTRODUCTION

When we were writing *Paleo Comfort Foods,* life was … shall we say … chaotic. We were both holding down full-time jobs, running and coaching at our gym morning and night, and trying to keep our house together, along with writing, editing and marketing the book. There were nights when we'd come home from work or the gym exhausted, with hours of editing left to do, and then we'd realize we needed to eat something. While yes, we're pretty certain that much of our budget went into our friends' pockets over at nearby restaurant Muss & Turner's, we did everything in our power to keep our dining-out budget reasonable. So on those nights when we found ourselves hungry and tired, we weren't about to spend two hours in the kitchen. We needed and wanted something quick, easy and delicious that still fit into our Paleo way of life.

One of the chief complaints we hear from clients at our gym and from others adopting a Paleo lifestyle is, "I don't have time to cook." Very often, these are the same people who post on Facebook about what happened on the latest episode of (insert name of favorite TV show here), or who can't seem to stop posting on Facebook, period! We're not saying that everyone has an extra ten hours a week to spend in the kitchen, as we know that in many families that is not possible or practical. However, with some shortcuts here and there, we're firm believers that with some time devoted to the kitchen versus, say, the television or internet, good, healthy, delicious food is possible, many times in forty-five minutes or less from start to finish!

The recipes in *Quick & Easy Paleo Comfort Foods* are just that: quick and easy. Ever since we welcomed our son, Scott, into the world, "quick and easy" has become an absolute necessity with regards to our meals, especially since we never know when he might cut a nap short! These recipes are tried and true and have all been made while juggling our lives and our newborn. It was our desire to share these recipes and concepts with you so that whether you're wiped out from a long day at work and don't want to invest a bunch of time in the kitchen or you're needing to whip up something fast to feed yourself and your family, you'll have lots of delicious

choices at your fingertips. Our goal is to provide you with some comfort food dishes that you can cook for your family in minutes, while not sacrificing flavor for time.

We'll provide you with ideas along the way to make things even easier and sometimes quicker, along with tips for enhancing the flavor on that rare night when you happen to have a few extra minutes on your hands. As we don't cook every single meal every single day from scratch, we'll also give you some ideas on saving your leftovers. And we'll show you how to use a sauce to convert something mundane into something incredibly flavorful and delicious. For the most part, we have tried to keep things as simple as possible—minimizing the number of recipes that call for the grill, fancy cooking techniques, or long and involved steps.

While we absolutely believe in slow cookers, braising things in the oven and smoking something on the grill for hours on end when you have time, this book is all about minimizing your time cooking and planning, while maximizing your health and filling your family with great-tasting food!

Happy eating!
Julie and Charles (and baby Scott!)

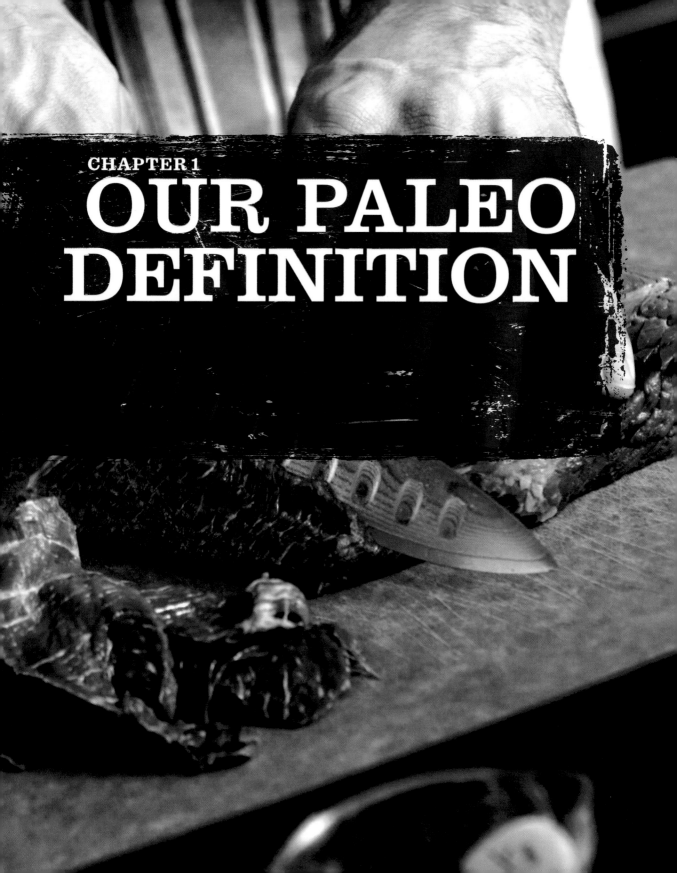

CHAPTER 1

OUR PALEO DEFINITION

If you're new to the Paleo way of life, welcome! If you're a seasoned Paleo vet, feel free to skip over this part. But for those who are just starting to explore the Paleo lifestyle, we thought it useful to share our definition of *Paleo* from a food perspective as those principles are what guided us in creating this book—and they work for us. (There are lots of other facets to living a Paleo lifestyle—like sleep, stress reduction, fitness. But that's a whole other book!) A slight caveat here: we are not physicians, nutritionists or evolutionary biologists, nor do we hold an advanced degree in topics intimately connected to the Paleo way of life. Fortunately, there are a bunch of people out there who do have extensive backgrounds in such topics, and we'll tell you a bit more about them later.

The interesting thing here to us is that if you poll ten people who profess to follow a Paleo lifestyle, chances are you'll get ten different answers as to what the definition of *Paleo* is. What's great about the Paleo lifestyle is that it's open to interpretation and individualization. It isn't black and white. What works for some people on their Paleo path might not work for others.

Generally speaking, our loose definition of *Paleo* is pretty simple: eat real foods—foods you grew in a garden, you picked from a tree, and you hunted, gathered or foraged. Our definition is not driven by a "Did a caveman eat this?" mentality, because a caveman did not have a food processor, an Apple computer or a stove like ours. Trying to live like a caveman isn't our intention. That being said, absolutely, there are some evolutionary reasons as to why we feel eating the Paleo way just makes sense. The overly processed "foodstuffs" found in grocery stores, which will look the same a year from now as they do today, thanks to a litany of preservatives, don't make us healthier. Instead, they've made our population sicker and fatter. This is why we think it best to stick with real food as much as possible.

Digging a little deeper, you can narrow down the Paleo definition of *real foods* to meats, seafood, fowl, eggs, vegetables, fruits, nuts, seeds and fats. From there, we can then look at what's good, what's even better, and what's best. When we work with clients at our gym, we talk to them about what's realistic with their budgets and lifestyle, and provide them with a hierarchy to help them choose the best options for them. For example, organic meats and poultry are better than conventionally raised meat and poultry that are treated with antibiotics, but the best choice would be grass-fed meats and pastured poultry from a local farm (many of which subscribe to organic practices, don't use hormones and antibiotics, and so on). We know such "best choices" aren't always available or reasonable, but with this hierarchy you can still be making good choices, which are far better than overly processed junk foods. What we advise our clients to do is make the best possible choices in their given situation. If someone cannot afford grass-fed beef, we'd rather they choose conventional beef over boxed macaroni and cheese. The last thing we want is for families to feel as though they cannot make the "best" choice, and then, therefore, ditch the entire concept of Paleo and go back to eating foods with ingredients lists that you'd need an advanced degree just to pronounce. Do the best you can with the choices available to you, and within your budget. Maybe move some things around in the budget so that, for example, you're paying less per month for cable TV and a little more for groceries.

WHAT TO EAT

People often think of Paleo as being so restrictive, but as you can see, there are a ton of foods to choose from when eating Paleo! We've listed what we consider to be the best choices within each food category.

PROTEIN

Red Meat and Game: Beef, buffalo, deer, lamb, goat, etc. Choose grass-fed, grass-finished local meats whenever possible.

Poultry: Chicken, turkey, duck, etc. Choose pastured, free-range local poultry, if possible. As an aside, chicken labeled "vegetarian" is not really a good thing (kind of like cows being corn-fed is not a good thing). Contrary to popular belief, chickens are not vegetarians!

Pork: Choose pastured, antibiotic-free local pork when possible.

Fish and Seafood: Salmon, albacore tuna, yellowfin tuna, cod, Pacific halibut, striped bass, clams, mahimahi, etc. Wild-caught is typically best, and you also should be conscious of sustainability and environmental contaminants. Check out the Monterey Bay Aquarium's Seafood Watch (www.montereybayaquarium.org) for helpful information on the most sustainable and safest choices.

Eggs: Ideally, eat eggs from pastured, free-range, antibiotic-free hens. Many people are now raising their own chickens for eggs, which is a great way to ensure your eggs aren't from chickens eating a bunch of soy or other things that aren't part of their natural diet!

FRUITS AND VEGGIES (AKA CARBOHYDRATES)

When some people hear about a Paleo diet, they often ask, "But where do you get your carbohydrates?" While yes, bread and cereals are very high in carbohydrates, fruits and vegetables are also carb sources—some with a higher carb content than others. A Paleo diet by design is not super low carb, but if very few fruits and vegetables are eaten, it can be low carb.

In terms of selecting fruits and vegetables, we highly suggest eating what's in season, when it's available, and buying from your local farms. When that's not possible, just do the best you can! This list does not include absolutely every fruit and vegetable out there—just some of the more commonly found ones. If you chose a different vegetable from this list each day, you'd still have great variety in your meals!

THE DIRTY DOZEN AND THE CLEAN 15

The Environmental Working Group (EWG) has classified twelve produce items as the "Dirty Dozen," because they are commonly contaminated with pesticides. We've marked the fruits and vegetables that belong to the Dirty Dozen with an *. We suggest you buy organic versions of these if at all possible! We have also marked produce that belongs to the EWG's "Clean 15" list with a +. These are the fruits and veggies deemed lowest in pesticides. If budgeting is a concern, you're likely safe choosing nonorganic versions of the Clean 15. (Note that this list is based on the 2012 guidelines and only Paleo-friendly foods are included here.)

Apples* (all varieties)

Apricots

Artichokes

Asparagus+

Avocados+ (Avocados are more fat than carbohydrate, so you'll see them listed in the fats section, too!)

Bananas

Beets

Bell peppers*

Blackberries

Blueberries

Bok choy

Broccoli

Brussels sprouts

Cabbage (red, green, Chinese)+

Cantaloupe (domestic)+

Carrots

Cauliflower

Celeriac

Celery*

Cherries*

Collards

Cucumbers

Daikon

Eggplant+

Fennel

Figs

Garlic

Grapefruit+

Grapes (imported)*

Jicama

Kale

Kiwi+

Kohlrabi

Lemons

Lettuce*

Limes

Mangoes+

Mushrooms+

Nectarines*

Okra

Onions+

Peaches*

Pears*

Pineapple+

Pumpkin

Radishes

Raspberries

Rhubarb

Spinach*

Squash (summer and winter: yellow, zucchini, spaghetti, butternut, acorn, delicata, etc.)

Strawberries*

Sweet potatoes+

Tomatoes

Watermelon+

FATS

Quality does matter here, so when you can be choosy about your fat sources, we always suggest going with the grass-fed, organic kinds.

Almonds, almond flour and almond butter (We prefer Honeyville blanched almond flour to other brands.)

Avocado oil

Avocados

Brazil nuts

Coconut, coconut milk and coconut oil (For coconut milk, we're talking the canned, full-fat unsweetened kind. Some of the brands in the boxes in your store's refrigerator section are full of all kinds of junk. However, Aroy-D does package coconut milk in a carton that has no additives, and it is a decent choice.)

Ghee (clarified butter) or regular butter (For those who can tolerate the milk solids in butter, regular butter from grass-fed cows is a fine choice.)

Hazelnuts (filberts) and hazelnut butter

Lard

Macadamia nuts, macadamia nut butter and macadamia nut oil

Olives and olive oil

Pecans and pecan butter

Sunflower seeds and sunflower seed butter

Tahini (sesame seed paste)

Tallow

Walnuts

What you won't see on a Paleo menu is gluten, grains, legumes, dairy (except butter, in some cases, for those who don't have adverse reactions to it), processed foods and sugars, and alcohol. (Oh, and you'll notice peanuts aren't on the list of fats. That's because they're actually legumes, not tree nuts. We just wanted to point that one out!) There are countless resources out there that explain the nos, and we'll get to those expert resources in a minute. Essentially, much of it comes down to inflammation, and a diet rich in the foods listed above is great at keeping you healthy and keeping inflammation at a minimum.

NOTE: While the aforementioned protein, carbohydrate and fat sources are commonly referred to as good Paleo choices, that does not mean that all choices listed will work for everyone. We are all unique, our bodies are unique and we may react to certain foods in unique ways. Despite adopting a Paleo lifestyle, some individuals still struggle with allergies to certain foods. Some have a significant autoimmune condition that is aggravated by certain foods like eggs or nightshades (for instance, tomatoes, eggplant, peppers, etc.). Some may find that the denser carbohydrate sources aren't healthy or safe for their blood sugar levels. Just because a food is Paleo friendly doesn't mean that it agrees with everyone. This is why it is so important to tinker with your diet to discover what works for you in your life. Be aware of those foods that you react poorly to or those you don't care for, and keep them off your list. Make your own food matrix of the protein, carbs and fats that you like, and use those frequently!

LIVING THE PALEO LIFESTYLE

We don't claim to be 100 percent Paleo all the time (dark chocolate is clearly not Paleo, nor is wine or tequila, and we sometimes indulge in those things), but we also don't go and chow down on gluten-filled doughnuts on the weekend. We are conscientious in our choices, and if and when we do go off the Paleo reservation, we own our choices and know such deviations might not make our stomachs feel great. This last statement speaks most clearly about what eating Paleo truly is...a conscious awareness that the things we put in our body have either a positive or negative impact on our health. Simply put, as our friends Dallas and Melissa Hartwig at Whole9 say, "There are no neutral foods."

Another deeply ingrained aspect of the Paleo lifestyle has to do with the relationship between our community and our food. You have already read, in several places, that we want you to buy as much of your food locally as possible. The connection between our community and the food we eat is something that has gradually deteriorated since the introduction of the supermarket in the early 1900s. But even back then many folks were still growing a substantial portion of their food. It was also much more common for the local grocery to be supplied by local farmers. It is our hope that we can begin to reconnect folks with a dying breed of amazing people—the American farmer. Supporting your local agriculture will reduce the environmental footprint of food transportation, will bring down the cost of these nutrient-dense foods for all consumers and will pour more money into your local economy...just to name a few benefits.

Don't get us wrong. We love the supermarket. We appreciate that some large chains are giving local produce a greater presence in their stores. Convenience is a reality today. With that in mind, remember, what you demand from your local grocery store is exactly what they will provide, or as noted in the documentary film *Food, Inc.,* every time we run an item past the supermarket scanner, we are casting our vote...for local or not, organic or not, processed or not.

Another endeavor we encourage everyone to try is planting a garden. Even the smallest of windowsill plants can yield delicious herbs all year round. Taking a small step toward sustainability will most likely save you money and most certainly give you a greater sense of being (not to mention tastier herbs!).

HERE'S A TIP: Rosemary will grow almost anywhere. Add a planter of thyme, basil, mint, parsley and oregano, and you have countless fresh options available to you for your next culinary adventure.

PALEO RESOURCES

There is a wealth of resources online to help you in your Paleo journey and better explain the why of eating and living this way. Truth be told, very often these folks have spent much of their lives researching these topics and are indeed experts in the field. Here are just a few places to start for information on the Paleo, or Primal, lifestyle:

RobbWolf.com: Robb Wolf is the *New York Times* bestselling author of *The Paleo Solution.* Robb's site offers forums, podcasts, guides to getting started and more, and is pretty much our go-to for Paleo resources and information. He has close to two hundred podcasts, covering everything from caloric restriction to Olympic weight lifting to pregnancy. There is pretty much no stone left unturned on Robb's site. Oh, and Robb got us started on this whole Paleo thing to begin with, so we might be only slightly biased.

MarksDailyApple.com: Mark Sisson is an author, athlete and all-around pretty incredible leader in the ancestral health community, and this is his website. Mark has published quite a few books on the Primal lifestyle, and they include not just commentary on what to eat (and how to cook it), but also considerations about sleep, play and life in general. Pretty sure we want to be like Mark when we grow up!

ThePaleoDiet.com: On this site, you'll find information from Dr. Loren Cordain—arguably one of the world's leading experts on the "Stone Age diet" in today's world. His website includes a significant number of links to published research concerning the Paleo lifestyle, and you'll also find links to the many books he's published on the topic.

Whole9Life.com: Dallas and Melissa Hartwig, authors of the *New York Times* bestselling book *It Starts with Food* and creators of the popular Whole30 program, run this popular website. Their blog posts, forums and workshops and the Whole30 community have helped thousands of people reframe their relationships with food, changing more lives than we can count!

AncestryFoundation.org: The Ancestral Health Society is concerned with human health and wellness from an ecological and evolutionary perspective. Their aim is to foster collaboration between scientists, health-care professionals and the general public. Every year, the Ancestral Health Society runs a popular symposium featuring top names in the Paleo lifestyle, and they post the presentations on their website for public access.

BalancedBites.com: Diane Sanfilippo is the *New York Times* bestselling author of *Practical Paleo,* one of the best books for people living a Paleo lifestyle. Her website includes recipes, podcasts, the incredibly popular 21-Day Sugar Detox Program, helpful guides on a wide variety of topics, and information on how to attend a Balanced Bites seminar. Diane is one of the leading voices in the Paleo community, and she has helped so many people make the transition to healthier living.

ChrisKresser.com: Otherwise known as The Healthy Skeptic, this site is full of information to help with the transition to the Paleo lifestyle, including specialized programs focused on fertility and pregnancy, tips on personalizing one's own Paleo journey, research on cholesterol, and much more. Chris is a licensed acupuncturist and has spent countless hours studying functional and integrative medicine. His blog posts and programs help people make sense of a lot of the research and conventional wisdom out in the world and what it all might really mean. Chris's website also features recipes, has a widely listened-to podcast, and is a fantastic resource for anyone and everyone living a Paleo or Primal lifestyle.

Of course there are a *ton* more websites, blogs, podcasts and books out there, but this seems like a good place to start. If you want even more info, go enter the word *Paleo* into the Google search engine, and you'll end up with plenty of websites, scholarly articles, personal blogs and more.

OUTFITTING THE QUICK & EASY KITCHEN

Now that we've outlined some of the particular foods you'll want to have on your shopping list, you'll need a few tools in the kitchen to help you cook up some delicious meals. We want you to arm yourself with some basic kitchen appliances, stock your pantry with commonly used ingredients, and pick up a few tips and tricks to make this journey a bit more pleasant.

TOOLS AND EQUIPMENT BASICS

Here are some of the tools we call for in the recipe instructions that will make your life a lot easier—and meal preparation quicker, too!

Microwave

Food processor

Knives (A quality chef's knife and a paring knife are essential, though a serrated knife is great for slicing tomatoes.)

Mixing bowls, measuring cups and measuring spoons

Glassware storage containers

Immersion blender

Cutting boards

Meat thermometer

Dutch oven or large saucepan

Small saucepan

Skillets and frying pans (cast-iron and/or stainless steel)

Several spatulas and wooden spoons

Cooking timer (if you don't have a smartphone)

PANTRY STAPLES

You'll want to have these staples on hand more often than not:

Almond flour

Bacon grease, lard and tallow

Balsamic vinegar, apple cider vinegar and white vinegar

Chicken stock and beef stock (Homemade is always best!)

Coconut aminos (good soy substitute)

Coconut flour

Coconut milk

Coconut oil

Garlic (Use fresh only. Don't use the jarred stuff that you keep in the refrigerator!)

Herbs and spices (assorted dried)

Olive oil

Tomatoes and tomato paste (canned), and other canned vegetables—be sure to check the labels for bad ingredients

HELPFUL TIPS AND TRICKS

Additionally, there are some things we suggest you keep in mind or choose to explore, as they will make your kitchen life even easier and meal preparation even faster!

+ **Take a knife skills course at your local cooking store.** The more proficient you are with knives, the faster your prep work becomes!

+ **Smaller and thinner things cook faster.** A ten-ounce piece of chicken is going to take a lot longer to cook than bite-size pieces. If you have a two-inch-thick piece of steak versus a one-inch-thick piece of steak, it's pretty easy to figure out which one will take longer to cook. If you're in a hurry, cut things nice and small!

+ **The saying "Many hands make light work" rings especially true in the kitchen.** Get spouses, kids and friends involved!

+ **Buy things already cut, washed and cooked.** A plain rotisserie chicken (not usually perfect Paleo) from the store can save you a bunch of time: you can shred the meat and then use the shredded chicken in many of the recipes. Most grocery stores carry all sorts of already chopped vegetables. Yes, it might be more expensive sometimes, but if it saves your sanity and precious minutes in your day, isn't that priceless?

+ **Chop one ingredient all at once,** meaning if you know you have other meals you're going to be cooking that same day or maybe later that week, do your chopping for all those meals all at once. Perhaps you know you're going to be using chopped onions or sliced bell peppers or cauliflower florets now and later in the week. Go ahead and chop that particular ingredient all at once, and store what you don't need at that moment in containers in the refrigerator. This makes things like a quick stir-fry or a scramble of sorts incredibly quick to put together (using what you have already chopped in the fridge).

+ **Cook extra of certain staples.** We cannot encourage this enough. The amount of time it takes to bake or grill one chicken breast or thigh is the same for two or three. Cook up extra portions of protein staples like these (they freeze well). That way you'll have the cooked meat on hand for making a bunch of different recipes.

+ **Cook extra, period.** Leftovers are the ultimate "quick and easy" meal. To spare yourself from cooking every meal every day and night, make sure you're making extra. Double or even triple recipes featured in this book, especially if you're feeding a big family, and freeze leftovers for future use (or eat the leftovers for breakfast the next day!).

+ **Make certain substitutions of ingredients to save a trip to the store.** For example, if you're out of beef stock, use some chicken stock instead.

+ **Remember: Perfect gets in the way of really good.** If a recipe calls for mincing something, you do not have to spend twenty minutes mincing the item perfectly. Save that for your cooking school exploits.

COOKING WITH THIS BOOK

Generally speaking, we tried to make the recipes as simple as possible. We also want to give you—the home cook—the flexibility to do things your own way. For example, very often we don't tell you the kind of fat to use to sauté things in, as everyone seems to have a different preference. We sometimes use bacon grease, sometimes lard, sometimes coconut oil and sometimes olive oil. We want you to know (and feel confident) that you can choose the fat that works best for you!

Yield: We learned with *Paleo Comfort Foods* that people like to have an idea how many servings a recipe yields. Here's the thing: A serving is not equal to all people. A petite, sedentary sixty-year-old woman is going to have an entirely different serving size than a twenty-two-year-old male CrossFit enthusiast looking to gain muscle. Generally speaking, in our house one serving is somewhere around four to eight ounces of protein. (This depends on what else we've eaten that day, our workout schedule, and so on.) As for veggies as side dishes, it depends on what else we're eating with the meal: are there other veggie side dishes, or are we filling up on that one? What we've provided are some general ideas as to how much a recipe yields, but how much someone in your house eats of the particular recipe is a very different matter altogether. Use "serving size" as a guideline, not an absolute!

Time: We've listed the approximate prep time and cooking time for each recipe, and that is the time it takes us, in our house, with our kitchen. Of course, every oven is going to cook slightly differently from the next. And the amount of time it takes for us to dice an onion may differ drastically from how long it takes you. But the times noted should still give you a pretty good sense of how long it will take to make each of these recipes.

Notes & Variations: We've tried to give you some ideas for tweaking these recipes, for giving them your own special flare, as well as some shortcut ideas and some helpful tricks.

Good luck on your journey to better health, more energy and oodles more fun in the kitchen. This book represents our effort to make the goal of nourishing your body, mind and spirit as attainable as possible. Now let's eat!

CHAPTER 2

STARTERS AND SNACKS

Bacon Jam 16

Curried Deviled Eggs 18

Jalapeño Poppers 20

Steak Skewers 22

Bacon- and Basil-Wrapped Shrimp 24

Clams Casino 26

Eleanor's Wings 28

Herb Crackers 30

Roasted Butternut Squash Dip 32

Rosemary Nuts 34

Basil-Bacon Tomato Bites 36

Tomato Tartare 38

BACON JAM

Yield: 2 cups

Bacon makes the world a better place. Locally made artisanal bacon makes it even more amazing. Perhaps one of the best culinary presents Julie has ever given me was a "Whole Hog" class with the folks from Pine Street Market in Atlanta. I spent two evenings with Rusty, the owner, learning to butcher a pig. In the process, we made bacon and several recipes, which have found a permanent place in our kitchen. This recipe was inspired by that class. We concocted a recipe very similar to this for our dinner that night. This jam is so good, you will have a hard time avoiding the temptation to just eat it with a spoon. And instead of gluten-filled bread, may I suggest spooning this over slices of an English cucumber as an appetizer? I also suggest joining Pine Street Market's Meat of the Month Club, and you'll get a pound of their amazing applewood-smoked bacon every month. — *CHARLES*

1 pound sliced bacon

½ teaspoon ground allspice

½ teaspoon cayenne pepper

Pinch of ground nutmeg

Pinch of cracked black pepper

¾ cup canned diced petite tomatoes

½ cup finely diced onion

¼ cup apple cider vinegar

¼ cup brandy (optional)

2 tablespoons honey

1 clove garlic, peeled and minced

1. Cut the bacon strips into very small pieces.

2. In a large saucepan, cook the bacon on medium-high heat for 10 to 12 minutes, or until the fat is rendered and the bacon starts to crisp.

3. Add the allspice, cayenne pepper, nutmeg and pepper and cook, stirring, for 30 seconds.

4. Add the rest of the ingredients.

5. Reduce the heat to low and simmer for 20 minutes, stirring occasionally.

6. Use a slotted spoon to scoop the bacon jam into a container, leaving most of the liquid behind.

7. Let cool to room temperature and serve however you choose.

15 **Active hands-on time**

35 **Total time**

NOTES: The brandy adds flavor and the alcohol in it cooks off, but you can certainly exclude it. If you make this ahead of time, store it in the refrigerator and bring it to room temperature before serving.

CURRIED DEVILED EGGS

Yield: 24 deviled eggs

There is a good chance you will find a deviled egg recipe in every book we ever write. There are so many different ways to prepare and enjoy these tasty treats. They are portable and keep well. We love taking these to parties as our "go-to" snack if there aren't other Paleo options available. It should be mentioned, hard-boiling eggs isn't as much art as it is science. If you live in a higher elevation, consider increasing the time you allow them to sit. Another option is to ask a local chef how long they hard-boil their eggs.

1 dozen large eggs

1 tablespoon white vinegar

½ cup Paleo Mayonnaise
  (see recipe page 204)

2 tablespoons chopped pickled ginger

1 tablespoon Dijon mustard

1 teaspoon curry powder

1 teaspoon apple cider vinegar

½ teaspoon mustard powder

¼ teaspoon cayenne pepper

Kosher salt, to taste

Several pinches of paprika, for garnish

1 tablespoon finely minced fresh chives,
  for garnish

NOTES: Store-bought hard-boiled eggs are a huge time-saver. A sandwich-size ziplock makes a great piping bag.

1. Place cold eggs in a large saucepan with the white vinegar. Cover with cold water to 1 inch above the eggs and bring to a boil.

2. Remove the eggs from the heat, cover and let stand for 12 minutes (or longer in higher altitudes). Drain and rinse eggs with cold water.

3. While the eggs are still warm, peel them.

4. Mix together the Paleo Mayonnaise, ginger, Dijon mustard, curry powder, vinegar, mustard powder, cayenne pepper and salt in a medium bowl.

5. Cut the eggs in half lengthwise and place whites on a tray while adding the yolks to the mayonnaise mixture.

6. Mash in the yolks with a large spoon and combine thoroughly.

7. Spoon the yolk mixture into egg whites or pipe using a piping bag.

8. Keep refrigerated until ready to serve and garnish with paprika and chives.

10 **Active hands-on time**

30 **Total time**

VARIATIONS: In a pinch, use ½ an avocado, mashed, or store-bought olive oil–based mayo instead of Paleo Mayonnaise.

JALAPEÑO POPPERS

Yield: 24 poppers

Our original recipe for these tasty treats involved a rotisserie grill and a little less work. The inspiration comes from the "rat toe" recipe our good friend, chef Todd Mussman, shared with me one evening. Todd also showcased the amazing Epicoa seven-skewer rotisserie his team won at the annual Cochon Heritage BBQ Festival contest in Memphis. Todd, along with fellow chefs Jay Swift, Nick Melvin and Tommy Searcy, brought home first place and some awesome gear. Knowing folks like these certainly has its advantages.

This recipe is an obvious adaptation. We figure most of you don't have a rotisserie lying around. If you are letting a little dairy into your Paleo lifestyle, consider grating some cheddar or jack cheese for the stuffing. A little cheese on these is the bee's knees. — *CHARLES*

1 dozen jalapeño peppers

1 pound shrimp, peeled, deveined and finely diced

¼ pound sliced bacon, finely diced

2 teaspoons sesame oil

½ teaspoon freshly ground black pepper

¼ teaspoon salt

NOTES: Wearing gloves is highly suggested when handling jalapeño peppers. One touch of the face, eyes or mouth will have you in some pain and a bit teary eyed, so don't touch.

1. Preheat the oven to 400°F.

2. Cut the peppers in half lengthwise and remove seeds. Place peppers faceup on a cookie sheet.

3. In a medium bowl, mix together the shrimp, bacon, sesame oil, pepper and salt. Combine well and spoon into each jalapeño.

4. Cook the peppers in the oven for 15 to 20 minutes, or until the bacon is cooked.

5. Allow to stand for a few minutes before serving.

15 **Active hands-on time**

35 **Total time**

STEAK SKEWERS

Yield: 12–16 skewers

We have a few "meat on a stick" recipes in this cookbook. It's as primal as eating comes. This is an easy recipe to scale up or down for guests or a hungry family. Be sure to have extra skewers soaking. You may need more if you are able to flex your knife skills and cut really thin slices of the sirloin. We prefer them a little on the thicker side to reduce the risk of overcooking the meat. If they are too thin, the meat could come out crispy.

1½ pounds beef sirloin, thinly sliced

12 to 16 bamboo skewers, soaked in water

½ teaspoon salt

1 teaspoon freshly ground black pepper

½ cup carrot juice

½ cup beef broth

½ cup water

2 tablespoons Worcestershire sauce

1 tablespoon coconut aminos

2 teaspoons balsamic vinegar

½ teaspoon onion powder

¼ teaspoon ground cumin

NOTE: It goes without saying, but we're going to say it, anyway: make sure your Worcestershire sauce (and any bottled sauces you purchase) is gluten free.

1. Preheat the oven to 450°F.

2. Thread the meat onto the skewers and sprinkle with salt and pepper.

3. Combine the remaining ingredients in a medium saucepan and bring to a boil over medium-high heat.

4. Reduce the heat and simmer until the liquid is reduced by half, about 10 to 15 minutes.

5. While the sauce is simmering, place the meat skewers on a cookie sheet and bake on the top rack for 6 to 8 minutes, depending on desired doneness.

6. Remove the skewers from the oven. Brush the meat with the sauce and serve.

15 Active hands-on time

30 Total time

BACON- AND BASIL- WRAPPED SHRIMP

Yield: 16–20 shrimp

This is a super-easy appetizer that's sure to please guests. We like using the larger shrimp for this recipe as it cuts down on labor and provides guests with a substantial bite. However, you could always go with smaller shrimp; just know that might entail extra prep time. If you're really pressed for time, buy your shrimp already peeled and deveined.

½ cup Barbecue Sauce
  (see recipe page 168)

1 teaspoon prepared horseradish
  (or more if you like more of a kick)

1 pound extra-large shrimp (16- to
  20-count), peeled and deveined

1 fresh basil leaf per shrimp (16 to
  20 basil leaves)

8 thin-sliced bacon strips, cut in half
  or thirds, depending on length

16 to 20 wooden toothpicks

 VARIATIONS: Instead of shrimp, large scallops or even boneless, skinless chicken pieces would be great in this dish. Then again, wrapping just about anything in bacon makes it hard to go wrong!

1. Preheat the oven to 375°F. Combine the barbecue sauce with the horseradish in a small bowl.

2. Wrap each shrimp with a basil leaf and then a piece of bacon. Try not to overlap the bacon, as you want it to cook evenly. Use a toothpick to secure the bacon in place. Arrange the shrimp on a baking sheet.

3. Place the shrimp in the oven and cook for about 5 to 6 minutes, or until they are just turning pink on one side. Remove the shrimp from the oven, turn the oven heat up to broil, and flip the shrimp over.

4. Place the shrimp back into the oven and broil for about 2 to 3 minutes per side, or until the bacon starts to get crispy.

5. Remove the shrimp from the oven, and baste all sides with the barbecue-horseradish sauce. Place the shrimp back in the oven under the broiler for about 1 to 2 minutes per side.

6. Remove the shrimp from the oven, baste one more time with the sauce, and serve hot with extra sauce on the side.

10 **Active hands-on time**

25 **Total time**

Bacon- and Basil-Wrapped Shrimp
with Barbecue Sauce (page 168)

CLAMS CASINO

Yield: 3 dozen clams

Clams casino has been a Sullivan family recipe for decades. I remember the first time I tried to order the same dish at a restaurant, expecting the same delight, and, man, was I disappointed to see bread crumbs detracting from the delicious topping! And not to mention the juices from the clams were nowhere to be had. In fact, this recipe was such a staple at my family's special occasions over the years that I gave the family recipe to the caterer on our wedding day. While I managed to chow down on only one clam that night, the fact that such a special family recipe was a part of our nuptials is something I'll never forget! — *JULIE*

2 tablespoons ghee (clarified butter) or fat of your choice

1 medium green bell pepper, seeded, deribbed and finely diced

1 medium yellow onion, peeled and finely diced

4 ounces pimento, finely diced

2 ounces dry white wine (or substitute chicken or fish broth)

3 dozen littleneck clams, cleaned and shucked

6 to 8 bacon strips, cut into 1- to 2-inch pieces (enough to cover all 36 clams)

1. In a small saucepan over medium heat, melt the ghee. Add the peppers, onions and pimentos and sauté until the onions are translucent, about 7 minutes. Stir in wine and simmer until most of the alcohol has cooked off, about 5 to 10 minutes.

2. Adjust the top rack of the oven so that it is about 6 inches away from the broiler flame. Preheat the broiler to high. Arrange the shucked clams on a baking sheet. Top each clam with 1-2 teaspoons of the veggie mixture (enough to cover the clam) and 1 bacon piece. (Place wider pieces of bacon on the larger clams. Remember the bacon will shrink!)

3. Broil the clams in the oven for 5 to 10 minutes, or until the bacon is crispy, but not burnt. Serve immediately and enjoy!

15 **Active hands-on time**

30 **Total time**

NOTE: If you cannot get your fishmonger to shuck the clams for you, plan on committing some extra time to this recipe to do the prep work.

ELEANOR'S WINGS

Yield: approximately 24 wing pieces

Muss & Turner's is one of our favorite restaurants in town and—lucky for us—is five minutes from our house. In 2012 the partners of Muss & Turner's (Chris, Todd and Ryan) opened Eleanor's, an almost speakeasy-type bar attached to Muss & Turner's. You literally walk through the restaurant to get to the "cooler door" to this space. The bar's namesake, Eleanor, is the controller for Muss & Turner's, Eleanor's and Local Three (another restaurant favorite of ours), as well as a faithful 6:00 a.m. member of our gym. While we absolutely love Eleanor and the bar named after her, we are pretty sure we love her a little bit more thanks to these wings. The original recipe calls for fifteen-plus ingredients for the spice blend.... We pared it down a bit but included those original spices as optional, should you want to go for the full experience.

FOR THE SEASONING:

2 teaspoons black peppercorns

2 teaspoons cumin seeds

2 teaspoons coriander seeds

¾ teaspoon fennel seeds

¾ teaspoon cardamom pods (optional)

½ teaspoon star anise (optional)

¼ teaspoon whole allspice berries

¼ teaspoon whole cloves

2 teaspoons garlic powder

2 teaspoons salt

1 teaspoon ground cinnamon

1 teaspoon unsweetened cocoa powder

½ teaspoon paprika

½ teaspoon cayenne pepper

½ teaspoon ground sumac (optional)

¼ teaspoon dried lavender (optional)

FOR THE WINGS:

3 pounds chicken wings, cut into drums and flats

1 tablespoon olive oil, plus 1 tablespoon for garnishing

Juice of 1 lemon

1. Preheat the oven to 500°F.

2. In a large skillet over medium heat, toast the black peppercorns, cumin seeds, coriander seeds, fennel seeds, cardamom pods, star anise, allspice berries and cloves. Place toasted spices in a spice grinder or a blender and grind. Pour the spice mixture into a small bowl along with the remaining seasoning ingredients and combine well. Set aside.

3. Place the chicken wings in a large mixing bowl and toss with 1 tablespoon of the olive oil and about 2 tablespoons of the spice mixture. Toss to coat well.

4. Place ovenproof metal cooling racks inside two sheet pans, and spread out the chicken wings evenly among the two. Bake for 20 to 25 minutes, turning once, or until the chicken is cooked through. The cooking time may vary based on your oven and how crispy you like your wings.*

5. Transfer the baked chicken wings to a large bowl and toss with the remaining olive oil, another tablespoon or two of the spice mixture and the lemon juice. Serve hot.

5 Active hands-on time

30 Total time

*If you like crispier wings and you have some extra time, before tossing the uncooked wings with the olive oil and spice mixture, bring a large pot of water to a boil and cook the wings for 10 minutes (this will render some of the fat). Pat the wings dry, and then proceed with step 3 above.

NOTES: This recipe will provide you with some extra spice mixture to have on hand, or if you'd like more, you can absolutely scale up the recipe to make sure you have a big stash of it on hand for other uses. We have coated chicken breasts and thighs with this spice mixture and have even roasted some cauliflower sprinkled with it.

HERB CRACKERS

Yield: approximately 2–3 dozen 1-inch crackers

We are big fans of using vegetables and even meat as substitutes for crackers and chips to accompany dips. (Hello? Have you ever tried dipping bacon in guacamole? It's eight shades of awesome.) Sometimes you just want a cracker, but without the grains and gluten. These crispy crackers do the trick and have even impressed non-Paleo people before!

2 cups almond flour

1 tablespoon plus 1 teaspoon olive oil

1 large egg

1 to 2 tablespoons minced dried herbs of your choice (oregano, rosemary, thyme, dill, etc.)

¼ teaspoon sea salt

Parchment paper, for rolling the dough

NOTES: These crackers will keep for a few days in an airtight container (provided you don't eat them all first). The dough for these crackers would also make a great pizza crust.

1. Preheat the oven to 350°F.

2. Combine all the ingredients in a medium mixing bowl.

3. Roll out the dough between 2 pieces of parchment paper to until it is ⅛ to ¼ inch thick, or your desired thickness. Remove the top piece of parchment paper only and, using a knife or pizza wheel, cut the dough into 1-inch shapes of your choice. Don't worry about separating the dough shapes. The crackers will be separated after baking. You could also use a cookie cutter or biscuit cutter to make other cracker shapes, but to do so you will need to remove the cut shapes from the surrounding dough, then repeat the process with the excess dough. Of course this would take a little more time!

4. Transfer the parchment paper with the dough shapes to a sheet pan or cookie sheet, and bake for 10 to 15 minutes, or until they are golden brown. Be careful not to burn the crackers. Allow them to cool before breaking them into individual crackers.

10 **Active hands-on time**

25 **Total time**

ROASTED BUTTERNUT SQUASH DIP

Yield: approximately 1 cup

Our inspiration for this recipe came from our friends at Muss and Turner's restaurant here in Atlanta. One evening they were serving a butternut squash hummus. It was made with chickpeas, so I passed on ordering it, but it got me thinking about what the sweetness of some roasted butternut squash might taste like with some tahini, lemon and garlic, and voilà! This recipe was born. You can serve this dip with a variety of vegetables or with some gluten-free crackers, like the Herb Crackers on page 30. — *JULIE*

1 small butternut squash, peeled, seeded and cut into ½ to 1-inch pieces (you will need 2 cups)

1 tablespoon olive oil, plus 2 tablespoons for dip

1½ tablespoons tahini

1 tablespoon freshly squeezed lemon juice

1 clove garlic, peeled and crushed

¼ teaspoon smoked paprika

Salt and freshly ground black pepper, to taste

1. Preheat the oven to 400°F. Place the butternut squash on a foil-lined sheet pan and drizzle with 1 tablespoon of the olive oil. Roast for 20 minutes, or until the squash is fork-tender, turning over halfway through cooking.

2. Combine the roasted squash, the remaining 2 tablespoons olive oil, tahini, lemon juice, garlic, paprika, salt and pepper in a food processor and blend until well combined.

3. Serve warm, or refrigerate and serve cold later.

NOTES: Pressed for time? Many grocery stores stock butternut squash that's already peeled and cut into pieces. Very often in the fall you can find butternut squash puree in some of the higher-end markets. It won't be roasted (so you won't have that same caramelized flavor), but it will still work well in this recipe. You could do the same with pumpkin puree. Because these purees might have a bit more water in them, you'd just want to add in your olive oil slowly, keeping an eye on the thickness to get your desired consistency—you may not need all of the olive oil.

10 **Active hands-on time**

30 **Total time**

VARIATIONS: Pumpkin or sweet potatoes would be fine substitutes for the butternut squash.

ROSEMARY NUTS

Yield: 1 pound

Back when I would help out in the kitchen at Sur La Table in Los Angeles, we once made this rosemary-nut mixture for a cooking class, and I recall all of us devouring it. I believe the recipe originated from the Union Square Cafe, if I'm not mistaken. I've since made these nuts countless times, and they are the perfect snacking food to have sitting around in small bowls at parties. Just be careful—it's very easy to eat far too many of these in one sitting! — *JULIE*

1 pound unsalted nuts of your choice (cashews, almonds, hazelnuts, etc.)

1 tablespoon ghee or coconut oil

2 tablespoons minced fresh rosemary

2 teaspoons honey (optional)

1½ teaspoons sea salt

¼ teaspoon cayenne pepper

 VARIATIONS: Want your nuts to have more of a kick? Add more cayenne pepper, or try some chipotle powder or ancho chili powder.

1. Preheat the oven to 375°F. Place the nuts on a sheet pan and toast for about 8 to 10 minutes.

2. Meanwhile, in a small skillet, heat the ghee or coconut oil over medium heat. Add the rosemary, honey, salt and cayenne and cook until the flavors are well incorporated and the ghee has melted, about 2 to 3 minutes. Remove from the heat.

3. Pour the nuts in a medium bowl and add the ghee mixture, stirring until the nuts are completely coated.

5 **Active hands-on time**

15 **Total time**

BASIL-BACON TOMATO BITES

Yield: 40-50 pieces (if using smaller tomatoes)

I've made these little "BBTs" (bacon, basil, tomato) for baby showers, birthday parties and more, and they are always a hit and vanish almost immediately. The only thing remotely time-consuming is the assembly, but it's oh so worth it! — *JULIE*

8 to 10 thick-cut bacon strips, cut into 1- to 2-inch pieces

10 to 12 fresh basil leaves, torn into 1-inch pieces

1 pint cherry, grape or Sungold tomatoes, halved crosswise

40 to 50 toothpicks

NOTE: Serve these bites with Quick Basil Mayo (page 192), a perfect dipping sauce.

1. Cook the bacon pieces in a large skillet or frying pan over medium heat until crispy. Drain on paper towels.

2. To assemble, place a piece of bacon and basil in between two halves of a tomato. Secure with a toothpick. Repeat with the rest of the tomatoes, bacon and basil.

10 **Active hands-on time**

20 **Total time**

VARIATION: If you're eating dairy, adding some mozzarella in addition to the bacon and basil would be so tasty, especially if it's drizzled with some olive oil and balsamic vinegar.

TOMATO TARTARE

Yield: 8-10 appetizer-size servings

This is one of the simplest, quickest, tastiest dishes we've ever made. It was inspired by our friends at Local Three—a great restaurant here in Atlanta—during one of their Paleo night dinners. We set out to replicate this one at home as a way to harness the great flavors of all the assorted tomatoes from our garden. Living in the South, we count ourselves lucky that our tomato harvest will very often last through October. What I find ironic is that growing up, I despised raw tomatoes, and now this is one of my all-time favorite summertime appetizers! — *JULIE*

1 pound assorted ripe tomatoes, seeded and minced

½ cup minced red onion

2 tablespoons capers, drained

2 tablespoons minced fresh flat-leaf (Italian) parsley

½ teaspoon salt

¼ teaspoon freshly ground black pepper

Good-quality olive oil, to taste (optional)

Balsamic vinegar, to taste (optional)

NOTES: You can absolutely peel your tomatoes if you'd like, but we don't find that the extra effort is really all that necessary. But go for it if you have the time! We like to serve this along with our Herb Crackers (see recipe page 30) or some sliced vegetables.

EQUIPMENT NOTE: We find that a serrated (bread) knife is a perfect knife for cutting tomatoes.

1. Combine the tomatoes, onions, capers, parsley, salt and pepper in a medium bowl and mix well. Cover and keep refrigerated until ready to serve.

2. To serve, strain off any excess liquid, and form into a round on a plate. To do so, place a metal ring (like a large biscuit cutter) onto a plate and fill the ring with the tomato mixture. Press the mixture down firmly to shape, using a paper towel to blot any excess juices. If you have remaining tomatoes, repeat this step on a second plate.

3. Drizzle with olive oil and balsamic vinegar, if desired, and serve.

10 **Active hands-on time**

10 **Total time**

CHAPTER 3

SOUPS, STEWS AND SALADS

Arugula Pancetta Salad 42

Brunswick-ish Stew 44

Clam Chowder 46

Shrimp Cobb Salad 48

Speedy Gonzales Chili 50

Cioppino 52

Chilled Melon Soup 54

Creamy Cauliflower and Chicken Soup 56

Creamy Tomato Soup 58

Greek Salad 60

Green Turkey Chili 62

Grilled Calamari Salad 64

Jicama, Pear and Grapefruit Salad 66

Sweet Potato, Spinach and Chorizo Stew 68

Tortilla-less Soup 70

Tuna Olive Salad 72

ARUGULA PANCETTA SALAD

Yield: 4 servings

Here is another recipe that came out of my "Whole Hog" class with Rusty and the folks from Pine Street Market in Atlanta. This easy salad recipe is one I adapted from my hog wild experience. Seek out the best-quality pancetta you can find, as that will take this recipe from good to great. — *CHARLES*

¼ pound pancetta, diced

1 tablespoon olive oil

1 tablespoon apple cider vinegar

Zest and juice of 1 lemon

1 teaspoon Dijon mustard

1 teaspoon honey (optional)

2 cloves garlic, peeled and minced

6 cups baby arugula (about 5 ounces)

1 cup cherry tomatoes, cut in half

¼ cup pecan halves, toasted (optional)

 VARIATIONS: Bacon ends (the chunks of bacon that are left after bacon is evenly sliced, which are often sold separately along with bacon pieces) can be substituted for the pancetta. You can use an orange instead of a lemon in the vinaigrette for a slightly sweeter taste, and spinach can be subbed if you don't have arugula.

1. Fry the pancetta in a large skillet over medium heat until the fat is rendered and the pancetta is crispy. Remove to a plate lined with paper towels.

2. Combine the olive oil, vinegar, lemon zest and juice, mustard, honey and garlic in a small glass bowl and whisk to combine.

3. Place the arugula, pancetta and tomatoes in a large serving bowl.

4. Drizzle the vinaigrette over the salad and toss to coat.

5. Garnish with toasted pecans, if desired.

10 **Active hands-on time**

20 **Total time**

BRUNSWICK-ISH STEW

Yield: 12 servings

Brunswick stew is normally a long and slow process, but it is always worth the wait. We've managed to deliver some lip-smacking flavor in a little less time with this method. Liquid smoke is a great product to keep on hand to replicate the smoky flavor (but without using the smoker). Keep in mind that a little bit of the liquid smoke goes a long way. You don't want to be heavy-handed with it. Plan on this one taking you a full forty-five minutes to make. This stew is very hearty and will crush those "chunky" soups in a can all day long.

1 tablespoon coconut oil

1 medium yellow onion, peeled and chopped

3 stalks celery, chopped

Two 28-ounce cans tomato sauce

One 14-ounce can diced tomatoes

1 medium green bell pepper, seeded, deribbed and chopped

1 cup Barbecue Sauce (see recipe page 168)

1 cup chicken broth

1 tablespoon Worcestershire sauce

1 tablespoon ghee

1 pound ground beef

1 pound pork tenderloin, thinly sliced

2 teaspoons liquid smoke

1 teaspoon cayenne pepper

1 teaspoon freshly ground black pepper

1 rotisserie chicken, shredded

3 cups Cauliflower Rice (see How to Make Cauliflower Rice page 45)

Tabasco sauce, to taste (optional)

Salt and freshly ground black pepper, to taste

1. In a large stockpot, heat the coconut oil over medium-high heat. Sauté the onions and celery until the onions are translucent, about 4 to 6 minutes.

2. Add the tomato sauce, diced tomatoes, peppers, Barbecue Sauce, chicken broth and Worcestershire sauce. Bring to a boil, and then reduce the heat and simmer, stirring occasionally.

3. Meanwhile, heat the ghee in a large skillet over medium heat and brown the beef and pork, breaking it up with a fork as it cooks, about 10 minutes.

4. Add the liquid smoke, cayenne pepper and black pepper to the meat to season it as you brown it.

5. Transfer the browned beef and pork to the pot with the sauce and then add the chicken and Cauliflower Rice. Simmer for 25 minutes.

6. You can add hot sauce and salt and pepper, if desired, when serving.

NOTES: Browning the meat ahead of time will speed things up. Feel free to use leftover meats from other recipes. As a shortcut, you can sub store-bought barbecue sauce for homemade. Just read the label to avoid excess sugar and gluten.

HOW TO MAKE CAULIFLOWER RICE

Cauliflower "Rice" is one of our favorite Paleo cooking tricks. It's healthy and delicious and incredibly easy to make. To start, prep your cauliflower, removing the green leaves and the core. Discard the leaves and core. Chop the cauliflower head into pieces that are small enough to fit into the feed tube of your food processor, and shred using the shred blade or pulse using the chopping blade until the cauliflower resembles small pieces of rice. (You can also shred the cauliflower by hand with a grater. You will want to keep your cauliflower pieces bigger, as they're more manageable to grate that way.) It's that simple! From there, you can steam the rice, fry the rice and serve it with dishes that call for rice.

15 **Active hands-on time**

45 **Total time**

CLAM CHOWDER

Yield: 5-6 main course servings

When I was a kid, one of our favorite family outings was to Friendly's. My mom, sister and I absolutely loved their sundaes (of course!) and, surprisingly, their New England clam chowder. (Personally, I think I loved putting loads of crackers in the soup, but that's a whole other point!) Chowders and the like at restaurants are typically off-limits to Paleo followers, as they are oftentimes thickened with flour and some form of dairy gives them their creaminess. Here we use pureed cauliflower along with coconut milk to achieve that same creamy texture. — *JULIE*

4 bacon strips

1 cup minced onion

2 cloves garlic, peeled and minced

3 cups cauliflower florets

1 cup chicken or fish stock

2 cups unsweetened coconut milk

2 cups clam juice

1 teaspoon dried thyme

Two 10-ounce cans clams, drained

Salt and freshly ground black pepper, to taste

1. Heat a large Dutch oven or soup pot over medium-high heat, and cook the bacon until crispy. Using a slotted spoon, remove the bacon to a plate lined with paper towels and set aside. Reserve the bacon drippings in the pot.

2. Add the onions and garlic to the bacon drippings and sauté until the onions are translucent, about 4 to 6 minutes. Add the cauliflower and stock, reduce the heat to medium, cover, and cook until the cauliflower is tender, about 8 to 10 minutes. Puree the onion-cauliflower mixture in a food processor or with an immersion blender until smooth.

3. Place the cauliflower puree back into the pot (if you used a food processor), add the coconut milk, clam juice and thyme, and simmer over medium-low heat for 2 to 3 minutes.

4. Add the clams and cook for 5 minutes. Meanwhile crumble the bacon. Season the chowder with salt and pepper and serve hot, topped with the crumbled bacon.

10 **Active hands-on time**

25 **Total time**

VARIATIONS: If you miss having potatoes in your chowder, dice up some additional cauliflower into small bites to mimic potatoes and add them in step 3. Alternatively, if you are okay with potatoes in your Paleo journey, feel free to add those in as you see fit, or maybe add some sweet potatoes for a slightly sweet flavor.

SHRIMP COBB SALAD

Yield: 4 servings

Not many salads make your house smell so good. This salad features bacon followed closely by shrimp and then some lemony goodness for the dressing. We brought a mess of Gulf shrimp home from our last trip to Mobile and needed something to do with all of them. Consider this our Gulf Coast spin on a classic chicken recipe. We really like putting the dressing exclusively on the greens to start. If you choose to mix it all together, great. If not, then you get to enjoy all the wonderful flavors of this salad individually.

4 bacon strips

1 pound extra-large shrimp (16- to 20-count), peeled and deveined

¼ teaspoon paprika

¼ teaspoon freshly ground black pepper

¼ teaspoon salt

2 tablespoons freshly squeezed lemon juice

1½ tablespoons olive oil

2 teaspoons Dijon mustard

2 small heads romaine lettuce, chopped or torn

1 cup shredded carrots

4 Roma tomatoes, sliced

4 large hard-boiled eggs, sliced

2 medium ripe Hass avocados, peeled, pits removed and sliced

¼ pound sliced ham, cut into ¼-inch strips

½ teaspoon Tabasco sauce (optional)

1. In a large skillet, cook the bacon over medium heat to render the fat. Remove the bacon to a plate lined with paper towels and let cool. Reserve the bacon drippings in the skillet.

2. Sprinkle the shrimp with the paprika, pepper and salt. Sauté the shrimp in the bacon drippings over medium heat until cooked through, about 5 minutes.

3. Blend the lemon juice, olive oil and Dijon mustard thoroughly in a small bowl to make a dressing.

4. Place the lettuce in a large bowl, pour the dressing over it, and gently toss. Arrange the carrots, tomatoes, hard-boiled eggs, avocados and ham atop the salad. Place the shrimp on top. (You may assemble individual servings or serve this family style.)

5. Chop the bacon into bits and sprinkle on the salad. Serve the salad at once with Tabasco sauce, if desired.

15 **Active hands-on time**

25 **Total time**

SPEEDY GONZALES CHILI

Yield: 6 servings

Chili can take as long to make as you want it to. The recipe in our first book is a keeper, but it called for nearly two hours of simmering. We've thoroughly enjoyed taking some of our standby recipes and finding a way to make them quicker. You can start this recipe at kickoff and be serving chili at halftime. Feel free to garnish with minced green onion, bacon bits or minced red onion. If dairy is something you're allowing in your life, this chili is great topped with some cheddar cheese.

1 tablespoon olive oil

1 medium yellow onion, peeled and chopped

1 tablespoon chili powder

1½ pounds ground beef

One 28-ounce can diced tomatoes

1 medium red bell pepper, seeded, deribbed and chopped

½ teaspoon onion powder

¼ teaspoon garlic powder

1. In a large saucepan, heat the olive oil over medium heat and sauté the onions until translucent, about 4 to 6 minutes.

2. Sprinkle chili powder on the beef, add the beef to the onions, and cook it, breaking it up with a fork as it browns, about 10 minutes.

3. Add the tomatoes, peppers, onion powder and garlic powder and simmer for 20 to 25 minutes.

10 **Active hands-on time**

40 **Total time**

CIOPPINO

Yield: 4–6 main course servings

This recipe was inspired by Robb Wolf and Nicki Violetti and pays homage to Nicki's Italian heritage. When we were on vacation together, they threw together this amazing cioppino in no time flat. We decided to re-create this dish when we got back home, the only difference being that we didn't have quite the same access to tasty fresh fish as we did when we were on vacation. No worries—Trader Joe's and many grocery stores have a great selection of frozen seafood to choose from. A bag of shrimp, scallops and calamari is a great choice for this.

2 tablespoons oil or cooking fat of choice

1 large yellow onion, peeled and finely diced

4 cloves garlic, peeled and minced

2 teaspoons dried oregano

1 teaspoon dried rosemary

½ teaspoon crushed red pepper flakes

One 24- or 25-ounce jar of your favorite tomato sauce (or one 28-ounce can crushed tomatoes)

1 cup clam juice

1 cup dry white wine (or substitute chicken or fish stock)

2 pounds assorted seafood of your choice (shrimp, bay scallops, calamari, halibut, clams or mussels, etc.)

1. Heat the oil over medium heat in a large Dutch oven or soup pot that is already hot, and sauté the onions until just translucent, about 4 minutes.

2. Add the garlic, oregano, rosemary and red pepper flakes and sauté for 30 seconds, or until just fragrant.

3. Mix in the tomato sauce, the clam juice and wine, and increase the heat to medium-high. Bring the sauce to a boil. Reduce the heat to medium and cook for 10 to 15 minutes to allow all the flavors to meld.

4. Add all the seafood and simmer until cooked through, about 5 to 7 minutes.

5 **Active hands-on time**

25-30 **Total time**

VARIATION: Should you prefer your cioppino more stew-like, you can also include seafood like clams and mussels in their shells, and increase the amount of seafood in this dish.

CHILLED MELON SOUP

Yield: 8 servings

I have been training Chris Hall, executive chef at one of the best restaurants in Atlanta (Local Three), for over a year. Despite his occupation, Chris has lost over eighty pounds by making the transition to eating Paleo and is seeing tremendous results in his physical fitness. He and his business partners have been so inspired by the results they have seen, they started a "Paleo night" every Monday at their restaurant. The inspiration for this recipe came from our second trip to their Paleo night, as this dish was featured that evening. And let me say, it was delicious! Take our advice: if you are ever in Atlanta, you simply must visit Local Three. These folks know a thing or two about great food and a phenomenal dining experience. — *CHARLES*

1 medium cantaloupe, peeled, seeded and cubed

½ cup unsweetened coconut milk

2 tablespoons freshly squeezed lime juice

2 tablespoons honey

4 teaspoons freshly squeezed lemon juice

¼ teaspoon ground cinnamon

⅛ teaspoon ground nutmeg

⅛ teaspoon salt

¼ cup sliced, pitted cherries

¼ cup pistachios, toasted

1. Place half of the cantaloupe in a blender and blend until smooth.

2. Add the remaining cantaloupe and all the ingredients except the cherries and pistachios and blend until smooth.

3. Pour the soup into bowls, garnish with the sliced cherries and pistachios, and serve at once, or chill until ready to serve.

NOTE: Buy precut melon to save time.

20 **Active hands-on time**

20 **Total time**

CREAMY CAULIFLOWER AND CHICKEN SOUP

Yield: 3–4 main course servings

This soup was the perfect comfort food for us as we headed into the winter, and we made several batches of this soup to freeze as we prepared for our baby's arrival. For those fearful of using coconut milk and having the dish taste like coconut, never fear, as you really cannot taste the coconut in this at all!

1 tablespoon oil or cooking fat of choice, plus 1 tablespoon for sautéing

1 pound boneless chicken breasts or thighs, chopped into bite-size pieces

1 medium yellow onion, peeled and diced

2 cloves garlic, peeled and minced

5 cups cauliflower florets

4 cups chicken stock

1 cup unsweetened coconut milk

1 teaspoon fresh tarragon, plus 2 teaspoons for garnishing

2 bacon strips (optional)

Salt and freshly ground black pepper, to taste

NOTE: To save time, buy already cooked chicken at the grocery store and eliminate the steps of cutting and cooking the chicken. It might not be pastured, but it still is a good choice.

1. Heat 1 tablespoon of the oil in a large Dutch oven or soup pot over medium-high heat. Add the chicken and cook for 4 to 5 minutes, or until the chicken is cooked through. Remove the chicken to a clean plate and set aside.

2. Add the remaining tablespoon of oil, and stir in the onions and garlic, sautéing for about 3 to 4 minutes, or until the onions are translucent. Add the cauliflower, the stock, coconut milk and 1 teaspoon of the tarragon. Bring to a boil, and then reduce heat to medium, cover, and simmer for 10 minutes, or until the cauliflower is fork-tender.

3. If opting for bacon, fry the bacon in a small skillet over medium heat until crispy while the cauliflower is cooking. Remove to a plate lined with paper towels, and break up into pieces.

4. Use an immersion blender to puree the cauliflower mixture until no lumps remain, or puree in a food processor or blender until smooth, working in batches.

5. Stir the chicken into the cauliflower mixture and simmer for 3 to 4 minutes to let the flavors combine. Season with salt and pepper to your liking.

6. Serve hot, garnished with the remaining 2 teaspoons tarragon and the bacon, if desired.

15 **Active hands-on time**

30 **Total time**

CREAMY TOMATO SOUP

Yield: 4–6 appetizer-size servings

Cream is a bit of a misnomer in this title, as in fact there is no cream in this recipe. Instead, coconut milk adds a velvety, creamy texture to this soup, miraculously without adding any coconut flavor. This soup is perfect to have on hand for those chilly fall or winter days. Top with some grilled chicken or shrimp to transform it into a one-dish meal.

2 tablespoons oil or cooking fat of choice

1 large onion, peeled and chopped

4 cloves garlic, peeled and coarsely chopped

One 28-ounce can crushed, diced or whole peeled tomatoes (San Marzano or home canned are best!)

1½ cups chicken stock (use vegetable stock if making vegetarian)

1 cup unsweetened coconut milk

2 tablespoons minced fresh basil, plus 1 tablespoon for garnishing

1 tablespoon tomato paste

1 tablespoon balsamic vinegar

NOTES: Hot liquids and blenders can be a very dangerous thing! As hot liquids will expand when blended, you want to make sure not to fill up your blender too high, and always cover the lid of the blender with a dish towel, pressing down firmly on the lid, to keep any escaping liquid from splattering all over your kitchen!

1. In a large Dutch oven or soup pot that is already hot, heat the oil over medium heat. Add the onions, and sauté until just about translucent, about 4 minutes. Stir in the garlic and sauté for 1 minute more.

2. Mix in the remaining ingredients, and simmer for 5 to 10 minutes to allow the flavors to meld.

3. Carefully pour a cup or two of the soup mixture into a blender (until it is only halfway full) and puree until smooth. Remove to a separate soup pot or container, and repeat with the remaining soup mixture, working in batches. Alternatively, you can use an immersion blender to puree the soup mixture.

4. Serve hot, topped with some minced basil for garnish.

15 **Active hands-on time**

20 **Total time**

GREEK SALAD

Yield: 6–8 small salad servings

Believe it or not, a traditional Greek salad doesn't usually involve lettuce. It's typically just tomatoes, cucumbers, onion, feta cheese, olives, seasonings and olive oil. The Americanized version often includes all of the above, along with lettuce and, depending upon where you are, a variety of other ingredients. That's the great thing about salads: you can add in whatever ingredients you like to make your own interpretation!

FOR THE DRESSING:

2 cloves garlic, peeled, crushed and minced

2 tablespoons red wine vinegar

1 tablespoon freshly squeezed lemon juice

1 teaspoon dried oregano

½ teaspoon Dijon mustard

½ teaspoon dried basil

½ cup olive oil

FOR THE SALAD:

1 large head romaine lettuce, chopped or leaves torn into pieces

1 large English cucumber, halved and cut into ¼-inch slices

4 to 5 Roma tomatoes, cut into wedges

1 small red onion, peeled and sliced very thin

1 cup pitted kalamata or other black olives

1. Combine all the dressing ingredients except the olive oil in a small bowl and whisk. Whisk in the olive oil, mixing thoroughly. Alternatively, you could use a blender or a Magic Bullet to make the dressing. Set aside.

2. Combine all the salad ingredients in a large bowl and toss with the dressing. Feel free to use less dressing, if desired. Serve immediately.

 VARIATIONS: Feta cheese is something you'll find in most restaurant-style Greek salads. If dairy is something you tolerate well, feel free to add some feta to your salad. Many restaurants serve Greek salad with peperoncini or bell peppers. If those appeal to you, definitely add some to your salad. To make this a meal, simply add some grilled protein of your choice and off you go!

10 **Active hands-on time**

10 **Total time**

GREEN TURKEY CHILI

Yield: 6–8 main course servings

We made quite a few batches of this to freeze in preparation for the arrival of our baby. Yes, there were days when we ate this chili at breakfast, lunch and dinner. The butternut squash adds a subtle sweetness to the chili, playing off the salty flavors of the other ingredients.

2 tablespoons oil or cooking fat of choice, plus 1 tablespoon for sautéing

2 pounds ground turkey or chicken

1 medium yellow onion, peeled and chopped

2 poblano peppers, seeded and minced

1 fresh jalapeño pepper, seeded and minced

5 cloves garlic, peeled and minced

One 28-ounce can tomatillos

2 cups chicken stock

1 pound butternut squash, peeled, seeded and chopped into bite-size pieces (2 cups)

Juice of 1 lime

2 teaspoons ground cumin

2 teaspoons chipotle powder

1 teaspoon dried oregano

2 tablespoons minced fresh cilantro (optional)

1. Heat 2 tablespoons of the oil in a large Dutch oven or soup pot over medium heat.

2. Add the ground turkey, and cook completely, breaking it up with a fork as it browns, about 10 minutes. Remove the turkey to a bowl or a plate.

3. Add the remaining 1 tablespoon of oil to the pot, stir in the onions, poblanos and jalapeños, and cook until the onions are translucent and the peppers are slightly softened, about 4 to 6 minutes. Add the garlic and cook 1 minute more.

4. Add the browned turkey to the pot, along with the tomatillos, chicken stock, squash, lime juice, cumin, chipotle powder and oregano, and cook for approximately 8 to 10 minutes, or until butternut squash is cooked through.

5. Serve garnished with cilantro, if desired.

 VARIATION: Don't have or like ground turkey? Feel free to use any ground meat of your choosing instead.

20 Active hands-on time

25–30 Total time

NOTE: To save time, microwave the butternut squash pieces in a bowl for about 6 to 8 minutes (while browning the meat or sautéing the onions and peppers) to cook it before adding it to the chili. Then reduce the cooking time in step 4 to three to four minutes to allow the flavors to meld.

GRILLED CALAMARI SALAD

Yield: 3–4 main course servings

We know that calamari tentacles send some people running for the hills, but as firm believers in diversifying our seafood choices, we're fans. Calamari is a great protein choice in that it's relatively inexpensive, it's almost always wild caught and sustainable, and it's chock-full of great vitamins and minerals, including B vitamins, selenium, zinc, magnesium, and so on.

2 tablespoons extra-virgin olive oil, plus 2 tablespoons for salad

2 tablespoons fresh squeezed lemon juice, plus 1 tablespoon for salad

2 cloves garlic, peeled and minced

¼ teaspoon crushed red pepper flakes

1 pound baby calamari, rinsed and drained

1 tablespoon red wine vinegar

3 Roma tomatoes, seeded and chopped

¼ cup chopped fresh flat-leaf (Italian) parsley

2 tablespoons minced kalamata olives

1 tablespoon capers, rinsed and drained

4 cups arugula (or salad greens of your choice)

Kosher salt and freshly ground black pepper, to taste

NOTE: Some markets label their calamari "baby squid." Yes, calamari is a member of the squid family, but not all squid is calamari!

1. In a medium bowl, combine 2 tablespoons of the oil, 2 tablespoons of the lemon juice, garlic and red pepper flakes. Add the calamari, mixing well. Allow to marinate for 5 minutes.

2. Meanwhile, preheat a grill pan over high heat. Once the pan is hot (to test the heat, sprinkle a few drops of water on the pan, and if they spatter, it's hot enough), place the calamari on the grill surface in a single layer. Grill 2 minutes per side, being careful not to overcook so the calamari does not get too chewy.

3. Remove the calamari to a clean medium bowl, and stir in the remaining 2 tablespoons olive oil, 1 tablespoon lemon juice and red wine vinegar. Fold in the tomatoes, parsley, olives and capers.

4. Arrange the arugula on individual plates. Spoon the calamari mixture on top, and season with salt and pepper, if desired.

5 **Active hands-on time**

10 **Total time**

VARIATION: If you don't want to use calamari, you could make this recipe with diced-up shrimp or scallops and it would still be mighty tasty!

JICAMA, PEAR AND GRAPEFRUIT SALAD

Yield: 3-4 side servings

Amazingly light and fresh, this salad goes great with seafood, chicken and pork. The jicama adds a great crunch, the pears add a hint of sweetness, and the grapefruit gives this just enough tanginess. This salad is a great one to bring along to a summertime picnic, too!

1 red grapefruit

3 or 4 ripe pears, cored and sliced thin

1 small jicama, peeled and julienned

¼ cup minced fresh mint leaves

2 tablespoons freshly squeezed lime juice (from about 1 lime)

2 tablespoons olive oil

½ teaspoon salt

¼ teaspoon cayenne pepper

1. Cut the peel and the pith from the grapefruit. Slice along the membranes to release the grapefruit segments. Cut each segment into small bites.

2. In a medium bowl, combine the pears, jicama, mint, lime juice, olive oil, salt and cayenne pepper and mix well. Fold in the grapefruit pieces.

 VARIATIONS: Get creative with what you decide to use here. Blood oranges instead of grapefruit would make this even sweeter and brighter. Mangoes would also make this salad particularly sweet and tangy.

 15 **Active hands-on time**

15 **Total time**

SWEET POTATO, SPINACH AND CHORIZO STEW

Yield: 3–4 main course servings

The flavor combination of sweet, smoky and spicy will never get old in this house. A smoky and spicy sausage like chorizo combined with sweet potatoes is something you'll see time and time again in dishes like breakfast hash, and it's just so hard to go wrong with that. Another bonus to soups and stews like this one is that they are a great way to "sneak in" additional green vegetables (like the spinach used in this recipe) for additional vitamins and nutrients.

1 tablespoon oil or cooking fat of choice

1 medium yellow onion, peeled and diced

2 cloves garlic, peeled and finely minced

4 small sweet potatoes, peeled and diced into bite-size pieces

1 pound chorizo links, cut into ¼-inch rounds (already cooked)

4 cups beef or chicken stock

4 cups fresh baby spinach

2 canned chipotle peppers in adobo sauce, diced (optional)

2 teaspoons ground cumin

2 teaspoons minced fresh rosemary

½ teaspoon dried oregano

1. In a large Dutch oven or soup pot that is already hot, heat the oil over medium heat. Stir in the onions and cook until translucent, about 4 to 6 minutes.

2. Add the garlic and sauté for about 30 to 60 seconds, or until just fragrant. Add the sweet potatoes and chorizo, and cook until just slightly browned, about 4 to 5 minutes.

3. Add the stock, spinach, chipotle peppers, cumin, rosemary and oregano and simmer until the sweet potatoes have softened, about 8 to 10 minutes.

15 **Active hands-on time**

25 **Total time**

VARIATION: If chorizo is not available where you are, use any link sausage you can find (though in our opinion, the hotter the better).

TORTILLA-LESS SOUP

Yield: 6–8 main course servings

I have a pretty big weakness for chicken tortilla soup, all but the tortilla, that is. I think some restaurants might use the soup as an excuse to get rid of stale tortilla chips, and I'm always quite happy to find a local restaurant that doesn't puree the corn chips into the soup. I find this soup is perfect any time of year, and I highly recommend keeping a vat of this in your freezer for when soup is calling your name! — *JULIE*

1 tablespoon oil or cooking fat of choice, plus 2 tablespoons for sautéing onions

2 pounds chicken (breast or thigh), cut into small, bite-size pieces

1 tablespoon fajita or taco seasoning

1 large yellow onion, peeled and diced

6 cloves garlic, peeled and minced

2 fresh jalapeño peppers, seeded and diced

1 large or 2 medium poblano peppers, seeded and diced (use more or less depending on how hot you like your soup)

2 quarts chicken stock

One 28-ounce can diced or crushed fire-roasted tomatoes

1 cup chopped fresh cilantro

Juice of 2 limes

Salt and freshly ground black pepper, to taste

Avocado slices, lime pinwheels and minced fresh cilantro, for garnish

1. Heat 1 tablespoon of the oil in a large Dutch oven or soup pot over medium heat. Add the chicken and fajita or taco seasoning, and brown until cooked through, about 5 minutes. Remove the chicken to a plate.

2. Add the remaining 2 tablespoons of oil to the Dutch oven, and sauté the onions until they are translucent, about 4 to 6 minutes.

3. Add the garlic, jalapeños and poblanos, and sauté for about 1 to 2 minutes, or until fragrant.

4. Pour in the chicken stock and the tomatoes and bring to a medium boil, cooking for about 3 to 5 minutes.

5. If you want a slightly thickened soup, strain out some of the tomatoes, onions and peppers, transfer to a blender or a Magic Bullet and puree. Pour the puree back into the broth.

6. Add the cooked chicken, cilantro and lime juice and stir. Season with salt and pepper to taste.

7. Serve the soup topped with avocado, lime and cilantro, if desired.

NOTES: To make this dish even faster, use already cooked chicken.

10 Active hands-on time

20-25 Total time

VARIATION: If you don't have fajita or taco seasoning on hand (always check your spice blends to make sure there are no not-so-great ingredients included), you can use a blend of chili powder, garlic powder and cayenne pepper as a substitute.

TUNA OLIVE SALAD

Yield: 3–4 main course servings

The tuna salad I grew up with was typically made with Miracle Whip and not much else, and it was served on Wonder Bread. It was cheap and easy, and the sweetness from the Miracle Whip made it something I liked (for the record, I don't like mayonnaise or anything like mayonnaise on its own). This tuna salad rendition pairs the freshness of the lemon beautifully with the tuna and the olives—no mayo needed, which makes me happy! — *JULIE*

15 ounces canned tuna, drained

¾ cup pitted kalamata olives, chopped

Juice of 1 lemon

3 tablespoons chopped fresh flat-leaf (Italian) parsley

2 teaspoons lemon zest

2 teaspoons good-quality olive oil

Salt and freshly ground black pepper, to taste

1. In a medium bowl, mix all the ingredients together until well combined.

2. Serve the tuna mixture on top of a green salad or eat it just as is!

NOTES: You can use any kind of olives that you'd like, but the briny flavor of the kalamatas works very well in this dish. To add more crunch, mix in some diced celery or apples, or any vegetables or fruits of your choosing.

5 Active hands-on time

5 Total time

CHAPTER 4

MAIN DISHES

Paella 77

Almond-Crusted Pork Tenderloin 80

Beef Kebabs 82

Egg Salad 84

Fried Chicken Tenders 86

Halibut with Cilantro Pesto. 88

Lamb Burgers 90

Macadamia Nut–Crusted Mahimahi. 92

Meat Loaf Muffins 94

Old-Fashioned Fiesta Omelets 96

Pan-Seared Sole 98

Pork Medallions and Peppers. 100

Quick Beef Curry. 102

Quick Skillet Frittata 104

Salisbury Steak 106

Seared Scallops with Onion-Mushroom Sauce 108

Stuffed Flounder. 110

Southwestern Shepherd's Pie. 113

Thanksgiving Burgers 116

Vegetable Meatza 118

Smothered Pork Chops 120

Baked Eggs with Vegetables. 122

Eggs Benedict Florentine. 125

Chicken and Broccoli Casserole **127**

Chicken Saltimbocca **130**

Chicken with Mustard Sauce **132**

Creamy Shrimp Fra Diavolo **134**

Ginger-Garlic-Scallion-Crusted Chicken **136**

Lamb Chops with Figs and Olives **138**

Lime and Coconut Chicken "Rice" **140**

Pan-Sautéed Steaks with Creamy Leeks and Mushrooms . . . **142**

Pork Chops with Tropical Salsa **144**

Quick Coq Au Vin **146**

Quick Roasted Whole Chicken **148**

Red Curry Chicken **150**

Sautéed Steaks with Tomato Pan Sauce and Wilted Arugula . **152**

Seared Salmon with Quick Pesto Mayo **154**

Spicy Salmon Cakes **156**

Steak Bites with Creamy Mushroom Sauce **158**

Stuffed Pork Chops **160**

Szechuan Stir-Fry **162**

PAELLA

Yield: 6-8 servings

Thought of by many as the national dish of Spain, paella, it turns out, is rather specific to the Valencia region of Spain. Though, if you go to any Spanish-inspired restaurant in the United States, chances are you'll find paella on the menu. While the word *paella* actually means "pan," the specific pan used most commonly to make paella is called a *paellera.* You will find all kinds of variations on paella, with some showcasing rabbit, chicken, duck, snails or beans, but typically you'll find that a paella recipe calls for saffron, olive oil and rice. Here we use our Cauliflower Rice instead, which not only is a bonus from a nutritive standpoint but also dramatically cuts down on the cooking time!

2 pinches of saffron threads

¼ cup hot water

2 pounds littleneck clams, live in the shell

2 tablespoons olive oil

1 large yellow onion, peeled and diced

1 large red bell pepper, seeded, deribbed and diced

1 large green bell pepper, seeded, deribbed and diced

4 cloves garlic, peeled and minced

3 cups Cauliflower Rice (see How to Make Cauliflower Rice page 45)

One 14½-ounce can diced tomatoes, drained

1½ cups chicken stock

2 teaspoons smoked paprika

1 pound large shrimp (26-30 count), in the shell

½ pound chorizo links, cut on the bias into ½-inch slices

15 **Active hands-on time**

30 **Total time**

1. In a small bowl, soak the saffron threads in the hot water.

2. Place the clams in a large bowl, cover them with fresh water and allow them to purge themselves of sand for 15 to 20 minutes, while you work on the paella.

3. Heat the oil over medium heat in a very large skillet or paella pan that is already hot. Sauté the onions for 5 minutes, or until almost translucent. Stir in the red and green peppers and garlic and cook for 2 to 3 minutes more.

4. Add the Cauliflower Rice, and combine well with the vegetables. Then add the saffron/water mixture, the tomatoes, chicken stock and paprika, stirring well. Allow this to simmer for 5 minutes to cook off some of the liquid.

5. Remove the clams from the water when they are done soaking, and discard any clams that remain open when tapped with your fingers.

6. Add the shrimp, chorizo and clams to the skillet or paella pan, and cook until the liquid has burned off and all the clams have opened. Discard any clams that don't open.

VARIATIONS: You can use any protein you see fit in this dish. Should you not wish to use seafood, use any meats of your choosing. Of course, you can also add any vegetables you'd like to create your own variation on this paella.

ALMOND-CRUSTED PORK TENDERLOIN

Yield: 6–8 servings

Quick, easy and so incredibly tasty. We like to leave whatever fat there is on the pork loin before we cook it (assuming you are using pastured pork, not factory farmed), as the tenderloin is very lean and doesn't have the rich flavor of fattier cuts. We find that the almonds add a bit more fatty flavor. We adorn this dish with a savory/sweet combination that ties together all the richness a pork entrée deserves.

1 large egg

2 pounds pork tenderloin

½ cup almonds, finely chopped

¼ cup coconut flour

2 teaspoons dried rosemary

1 teaspoon freshly ground black pepper

½ teaspoon garlic powder

½ teaspoon salt

2 teaspoons coconut oil, for coating the pan

1 tablespoon ghee

One 15-ounce can beets, drained and coarsely chopped

2 cups water

¼ cup seedless black raisins

¼ cup dried cranberries

1 tablespoon apple cider vinegar

1 tablespoon honey (optional)

½ cup cherries, pitted and chopped

1. Preheat the oven to 450°F.

2. In a large bowl, whisk the egg until blended and then place tenderloin in egg mixture to coat.

3. Combine the almonds, coconut flour, rosemary, pepper, garlic powder and salt in a small bowl and mix well.

4. Coat a broiler pan with the coconut oil. Dredge the pork in the almond mixture and place on the broiler pan. Bake for 20 to 30 minutes, or until the internal temperature is 145°F.

5. While the pork is cooking, heat the ghee in a medium saucepan over medium heat and sauté the beets until they have softened a bit, about 4 minutes.

6. Add the water, raisins, cranberries, vinegar and honey to the beets, cover, and bring to a boil. Boil for a few minutes.

7. Reduce the heat to medium-low and simmer until the liquid has reduced, about 10 minutes.

8. Stir in the cherries and allow the chutney to cool.

9. Remove the pork from the oven, cover with foil and let sit for 10 minutes. Slice the pork into ½-inch pieces. Spoon the chutney over the pork and serve at once.

20 **Active hands-on time**

45 **Total time**

NOTE: Frozen cherries work just fine for the chutney.

BEEF KEBABS

Yield: 6-8 servings

"Meat on a stick" is rather synonymous with the Paleo/Primal way of eating. Kebabs are also just fun to construct and are a great way to involve everyone in the dinner assembly, especially the kids. When possible, we like to prepare these a day in advance for things like tailgates, porch parties and small gatherings. It is incredibly easy to scale this recipe up to accommodate more guests.

FOR THE MARINADE:

½ cup olive oil

¼ cup coconut aminos

¼ cup honey

2 tablespoons red wine vinegar

3 cloves garlic, peeled and minced

1 tablespoon minced fresh ginger (optional)

FOR THE KEBABS:

2 pounds beef sirloin, cut into 1-inch cubes

1 large red or green bell pepper, seeded, deveined and cut into 1-inch chunks

1 medium red onion, peeled and cut into 1-inch chunks

8 to 10 bamboo skewers, soaked in water

NOTE: Welder's gloves make great grill and oven mitts. If you have more time, allow the meat to marinate longer.

1. Mix all the marinade ingredients together in a small bowl. Place the beef cubes in a large bowl and pour the marinade over them. Cover and refrigerate the beef for 20 minutes.

2. Heat an outdoor grill or an indoor grill pan to medium-high heat.

3. Remove the beef from the refrigerator and begin making the kebabs. Thread the beef, peppers and onions onto the skewers, alternating. Reserve the leftover marinade.

4. Place the skewers on the grill and cook for 6 to 8 minutes per side. Upon flipping them, apply the leftover marinade with a brush.

5. Allow the skewers to rest for a few minutes after you pull them off the grill and then serve.

25 **Active hands-on time**

40 **Total time**

VARIATIONS: You can add fresh pineapple chunks to the skewers for a bit of an island flair. Marinating the meat overnight infuses more flavor.

EGG SALAD

Yield: 4-6 servings

Egg salad is one of those recipes you can "overdo." We like to keep the ingredients simple. You will almost always find hard-boiled eggs in our refrigerator, as they are a perfect protein source (though Julie still doesn't like them). If you have hard-boiled eggs on hand (which I highly suggest), this meal becomes very quick to assemble. The addition of black olives to this lunchtime staple brings in just a bit of a briny taste to the dish. The scalability and versatility of this recipe make it a household favorite. You can prepare single servings or large quantities for entertaining with very little difference in prep time. — *CHARLES*

12 large hard-boiled eggs, peeled and chopped

1 cup pitted black olives, sliced

½ cup finely chopped white onion

¼ cup Paleo Mayonnaise (see recipe page 204)

1 tablespoon Dijon mustard

1 teaspoon apple cider vinegar

½ teaspoon garlic powder

Salt and freshly ground black pepper, to taste

NOTE: Store-bought hard-boiled eggs are a huge time-saver.

1. Combine all the ingredients except the salt and pepper in a medium bowl and mix well.

2. Add salt and pepper, to taste.

3. Serve on tomato or zucchini slices or lettuce leaves and sprinkle with additional pepper.

15 **Active hands-on time**

15 **Total time**

FRIED CHICKEN TENDERS

Yield: 6–8 servings

This is a great recipe for all ages. We make it often to show parents how to feed their kids a food they love in a much healthier way. You and the kids will be amazed at the flavor the pork rinds bring to this dish. If you are looking for something fun to do with your children in the kitchen, this recipe is a great place to start.

1 large egg

2 pounds skinless, boneless chicken breasts, cut into ½-inch strips

2½ cups pork rinds, broken into small pieces

½ cup coconut flour

1 teaspoon freshly ground black pepper

½ teaspoon salt

½ teaspoon garlic powder

½ teaspoon chipotle powder

½ cup coconut oil

1. Beat the egg in a medium bowl and place the chicken in it to soak.

2. Place the pork rinds, coconut flour, pepper, salt, garlic powder and chipotle powder in a food processor and pulse until the mixture resembles a flour.

3. Pour the flour mixture onto a large plate and spread it out.

4. Using a fork, individually coat each chicken strip with the flour mixture and set on a large clean plate.

5. Heat the coconut oil over medium-high heat in a large skillet.

6. Using tongs, place some of the chicken strips in the oil and cook each side for 3 to 4 minutes, or until golden brown.

7. Remove the chicken strips to a plate lined with paper towels to soak up the excess oil. Repeat with the remaining chicken strips, frying them in batches.

8. Serve at once with Avocado Dipping Sauce (page 166), or any sauce of your choosing.

15 **Active hands-on time**

35 **Total time**

HALIBUT WITH CILANTRO PESTO

Yield: 4 servings

We feature a triple crown of flatfish in this book—halibut, sole and flounder. Halibut is the largest of the three fish, and it will take longer to cook through. You also need to take care not to overcook this fish. To strike this balance, we give the fish a quick sauté to lock in the flavor and moisture, and then we finish it in the oven. You'll love the cilantro spin on pesto.

1 tablespoon ghee

4 halibut steaks (6 ounces each)

Juice of 1 lemon

2 cups chopped fresh cilantro

3 tablespoons cashew nuts, toasted

2 cloves garlic, peeled

¼ teaspoon salt, divided

¼ teaspoon freshly ground black pepper

½ cup olive oil

Freshly cracked pepper, to taste

NOTES: Lay the halibut steaks in the skillet slowly and give them a little wiggle to keep them from sticking to the pan. A food processor works just as well for the cilantro pesto. The stems of cilantro hold plenty of flavor, so don't waste time picking the leaves off the stems. Just use it all.

1. Preheat the oven to 375°F.

2. Heat the ghee in an extra large oven-safe skillet over medium-high heat and sauté the steaks, skin side up, for 2 minutes.

3. Flip steaks and pour lemon juice over each. Place in oven and cook for 5 minutes.

4. While the steaks are in the oven, prepare the pesto. Mix together the cilantro, cashews, garlic, salt and pepper in a blender. Slowly add the olive oil to the blender and process until smooth.

5. Remove the steaks from the oven and let rest for 5 minutes to finish cooking.

6. Crack fresh pepper over the halibut steaks and serve with the cilantro pesto.

10 **Active hands-on time**

25 **Total time**

LAMB BURGERS

Yield: 6 burgers

Lamb has such a unique flavor. Making burgers with lamb allows you to infuse so many different flavors into the burger. Lemon and especially mint are the quintessential flavors for a lamb burger. The hint of red onion pairs well with the lamb and you get to taste all of that in this delicious recipe. These are sure to be a hit and will bring a little Greek spin into an American backyard tradition.

1½ pounds ground lamb

2 large egg yolks

¼ cup finely diced red onion

2 cloves garlic, peeled and finely minced

Zest of 1 lemon

1 tablespoon minced fresh mint

2 teaspoons minced fresh rosemary

1 teaspoon minced fresh oregano

¼ teaspoon freshly ground black pepper

Pinch of salt

NOTE: While the grill is hot, slice what remains of your red onion into disks and grill to serve with your burgers. Also, consider making a batch of Tzatziki Sauce (see recipe page 182) to go on the burgers.

1. Heat the grill to medium-high heat (around 400°F).

2. Allow the lamb to come to room temperature while you do the next step.

3. Combine the egg yolks, onions, garlic, lemon zest, mint, rosemary, oregano, pepper and salt in a large bowl and mix well.

4. Add the lamb to the egg mixture and combine thoroughly. Form the lamb into 6 patties of equal size.

5. Grill the burgers for approximately 4 minutes on each side, or cook to desired doneness.

6. Serve on lettuce leaves with tomatoes.

20 **Active hands-on time**

30 **Total time**

MACADAMIA NUT–CRUSTED MAHIMAHI

Yield: 6 servings

One of these days, we'll be lucky enough to meet our fellow Atlantan Alton Brown. Alton is a brilliant cook and we draw great inspiration from his passion for "Good Eats." I adapted this deliciousness from a recipe of Alton's. Here's a little tip for all you Paleo eaters…if you like panko crumbs, you should really give pork rinds a try. They have some similar characteristics to panko and don't take you off the Paleo wagon. Maybe this recipe will earn us a guest appearance on Alton's next show? I'm not sure we are ready for *Iron Chef America* just yet, but we welcome the chance to hang with one of the greats.

1 cup macadamia nuts, toasted

1 cup pork rinds

2 tablespoons coconut flour

½ teaspoon freshly ground black pepper

¼ teaspoon onion powder

2 teaspoons coconut oil, for coating

6 mahimahi fillets

Salt and freshly ground black pepper, to taste

3 tablespoons ghee, melted

2 tablespoons unsweetened coconut milk

1. Preheat the oven to 425°F.

2. Pulse the nuts and pork rinds in a food processor and grind to a powder. Pour the nut-pork rind mixture into a medium bowl, and stir in the coconut flour, pepper and onion powder, combining well. Set aside.

3. Cover a cookie sheet with aluminum foil and coat the foil evenly with the coconut oil. Place the mahimahi fillets on the foil and sprinkle with salt and pepper. Bake for 5 minutes.

4. While the fish is baking, stir the ghee into the nut-pork rind mixture.

5. Remove the fish from the oven, liberally brush the coconut milk on each fillet and then coat with the nut-pork rind mixture. Pat down the coating to ensure that it adheres to the fish.

6. Return the fish to the oven and bake for 10 more minutes, or until the crust is brown.

7. Remove the fish from the oven and allow it to rest for 10 minutes before serving.

20 **Active hands-on time**

35 **Total time**

Macadamia Nut–Crusted Mahimahi with Root Veggie Cakes (page 210) and Sautéed Brussels Sprouts (page 214)

MEAT LOAF MUFFINS

Yield: 10-12 muffins

There is an added step to this recipe, which we think makes all the difference. With traditional meat loaf, you just adorn the top of the meat with ketchup, but we actually infuse our signature tomato mixture into the meat loaf itself. We think you'll agree that these "muffins" pack a flavorful punch. And the portability factor of these is nice and convenient. Meat Loaf Muffins are a handy snack for the busy person who's in a rush to get out the door. They're also perfect for kids' lunch boxes.

1 tablespoon olive oil, plus more for greasing the muffin tin

¾ cup finely diced onion

½ cup finely diced button mushrooms

½ cup finely chopped green bell pepper

¼ cup tomato paste

1 tablespoon ground mustard

2 teaspoons Worcestershire sauce

1 teaspoon finely minced fresh rosemary

2 cloves garlic, peeled and minced

¼ teaspoon freshly ground black pepper

1½ pounds ground beef

1 large egg

1 teaspoon dried thyme

½ teaspoon garlic powder

¼ cup carrot juice

¼ cup water

 VARIATIONS: Replace ½ pound of the ground beef with ground pork or venison to alter the flavor a bit.

10 **Active hands-on time**

40 **Total time**

1. Preheat the oven to 350°F. Grease the wells of a 12-cup muffin tin with olive oil.

2. Heat the remaining 1 tablespoon olive oil in a medium skillet over medium heat and sauté the onions, mushrooms and peppers for about 2 minutes. Remove from the heat and allow the vegetables to cool.

3. In a small bowl, combine the tomato paste, mustard, Worcestershire sauce, rosemary, garlic and pepper.

4. In a large bowl, mix together the beef, the reserved sautéed vegetables, egg, thyme and garlic powder. Stir in half of the tomato mixture and combine well.

5. Spoon the meat mixture into the greased muffin tin and bake for 10 minutes.

6. While the muffins are baking, combine the remaining tomato mixture, carrot juice and water in a small saucepan. Bring to a quick boil over medium-high heat, and then reduce the heat and simmer, covered, until the muffins are removed from the oven.

7. Remove the muffins from the oven and spoon or brush the sauce on each muffin. Place the muffins back in the oven and bake for another 15 minutes, or until the internal temperature is 160°F.

8. Allow the muffins to stand for about 5 minutes before eating.

NOTES: Avoid using paper muffin cups, as they will get soggy from the liquid in the meat loaf during cooking. If you end up with an empty muffin tin well or two, fill those halfway with water before placing the muffin tin in the oven to prevent it from warping.

OLD-FASHIONED FIESTA OMELETS

Yield: 4-6 omelets

"Old-fashioned" omelets were always my go-to order at Waffle House, and this recipe was inspired by my countless trips there. They are incredibly quick to make and you can throw anything in the middle of them. If you don't own a griddle, you can try these in a nonstick skillet. However, they make some very affordable griddles that you can use on your stovetop, and they really come in handy when you want burgers and it's raining. Rolling the omelets may take practice. Worst-case scenario, you still get to eat a tasty meal.

The options for the inside are unlimited. Don't go overboard with too much in the filling, or you will have a difficult time folding the omelets over. You are free to make the omelets bigger, but I suggest keeping them small until you have your technique down cold. If you eat dairy, consider adding a bit of cheese. — *CHARLES*

1 tablespoon butter, plus 2 tablespoons for greasing griddle

1 cup chopped onion

2 cups fresh spinach

½ cup sliced button mushrooms

1 cup diced ham

1 dozen large eggs

1 cup tomato salsa

NOTE: This recipe is just cause to get a long nonstick turner (sometimes called a spatula) with a large head and a griddle for your stovetop. Feel free to flex your skills and roll the omelet.

1. Preheat the griddle to medium-high heat.

2. Prepare the omelet filling. Heat 1 tablespoon of the butter in a large skillet and sauté the onions for two minutes. Then add the spinach and mushrooms and sauté for 2 more minutes. Mix in the ham and remove from the heat.

3. Thoroughly whisk together the eggs in a large measuring cup. Grease your griddle using portions of the remaining 2 tablespoons of butter with each batch. Fill a ¼-cup measuring cup with the eggs and pour onto the hot griddle. Make 1 or 2 omelets at a time, depending on the griddle's size. Immediately after pouring the ¼-cup eggs on the griddle, spread a portion of the filling over it.

15 **Active hands-on time**

20 **Total time**

4. Once omelet has set, using a long spatula, carefully roll the omelet over like you are folding a napkin.

5. Flip the entire omelet over once to allow it to cook through. Remove to a plate and garnish with the salsa. Repeat the process until all the omelets are made.

PAN-SEARED SOLE

Yield: 3–4 servings

What a delightful and simple recipe this is to prepare. We love our flatfish! Flounder and sole are flaky and light and cook up so fast. Try to find sole that is Pacific caught and more sustainable. We love this served over a bed of blanched greens. This is a fantastic breakfast option, seeing that it cooks up about as fast as eggs.

1 pound Dover sole fillets (or another Pacific sole)

Pinch of salt, plus more for seasoning cooked fish

¼ cup coconut flour

1½ tablespoons butter or coconut oil

1 teaspoon lemon zest

Freshly ground black pepper, to taste

4 lemon wedges, for serving

 NOTE: This dish would go great with our Paleo Grits recipe (made with cauliflower), as featured in *Paleo Comfort Foods.*

 VARIATIONS: Consider orange zest or wedges as an alternative to lemon. Can't find sole? You can substitute flounder or tilapia in a pinch.

1. Sprinkle the fillets with the pinch of salt and then dust with the coconut flour.

2. In a medium-size frying pan, heat the butter or oil over medium-high heat. Place fillets in the pan and cook for 1 minute.

3. Flip the fillets, sprinkle with the lemon zest and cook for another 1½ to 3 minutes, or until the fish is opaque in color.

4. Remove the fish from the pan, season with salt and pepper to taste, and serve at once with lemon wedges.

10 **Active hands-on time**

15 **Total time**

PORK MEDALLIONS AND PEPPERS

Yield: 4 servings

We love the simplicity of this recipe. Feel free to double the recipe if you have a skillet large enough to hold that much meat. Oh, and if you haven't planted a rosemary bush yet, now is the thyme (forgive the pun). Seriously, spending money at the store to buy an entire packet of rosemary is just silly. Rosemary grows nearly anywhere, it's an evergreen (so it will last through the winter) and it's a perfect decorative plant for your home. Not to mention that there are so few occasions where you need a whole packet of it at once (as sold in the stores). When you are done reading this recipe, it's time to start building your herb garden at home. If you don't have a green thumb, chances are good that you've just rubbed the green off using that smartphone for too long.

½ teaspoon kosher salt

½ teaspoon freshly ground black pepper

1 pound pork tenderloin, cut into 1-inch medallions

1 tablespoon olive oil

1 large red bell pepper, seeded, deribbed and sliced

1 large yellow bell pepper, seeded, deribbed and sliced

2 cloves garlic, peeled and minced

1 teaspoon finely minced fresh rosemary, plus 1 teaspoon for garnishing

1 teaspoon lime juice

2 teaspoons balsamic vinegar

1. Sprinkle the salt and pepper on the pork medallions.

2. In a large skillet that is already hot, heat the oil over medium-high heat and add the pork. Cook for 5 minutes and then flip.

3. Reduce the heat to medium, add the peppers, garlic and 1 teaspoon of the rosemary, and cook for another 8 minutes, or until the pork is cooked through.

4. Combine the lime juice and vinegar in a small bowl and pour over the pork. Top with the remaining 1 teaspoon rosemary.

5 **Active hands-on time**

25 **Total time**

NOTES: Never put oil or proteins into a cold skillet. Be sure that your skillet is hot when you add the oil and hot when you add the protein. This ensures that the meat cooks properly and you get a good sear on the outside. How do you test it? Sprinkle a little water in the pan as it heats. If the water beads up and rolls around in the pan, you are ready to cook. (For you science-minded folks out there, this is called the Leidenfrost effect.)

QUICK BEEF CURRY

Yield: 3-4 servings

If you read our first cookbook, *Paleo Comfort Foods,* you already know that we are big fans of curry. Julie introduced me to curry, and I contend it is one of the reasons I married her. One of the first meals I ever made for Julie was a fusion-inspired curry, which is in our first cookbook. We use cube steak in this "quicker" version because the protein cooks up faster. — *CHARLES*

1 tablespoon coconut oil

1 pound cube steak

1 cup chopped onion

1 medium red bell pepper, seeded, deribbed and chopped

2 tablespoons green curry paste

2 cups broccoli florets

2 cups sliced eggplant

¼ cup fresh whole Thai basil leaves

2 cups beef stock

1 cup unsweetened coconut milk

1 tablespoon fish sauce

2 Kaffir lime leaves, if available

3 cups Cauliflower Rice (see How to Make Cauliflower Rice page 45)

¼ cup water

12 whole Thai chili peppers, for garnish

1. Heat the coconut oil over medium heat in a medium-size Dutch oven. While the oil is heating, cut the cube steak into about 1-inch squares.

2. When the oil begins to smoke, add the meat to the Dutch oven and brown on all sides.

3. Add the onions, peppers and curry paste and sauté for about 3 minutes.

4. Add the broccoli, eggplant and basil and sauté for another 2 minutes.

5. Add the beef stock, coconut milk, fish sauce and Kaffir lime leaves and bring to a quick boil, stirring frequently. Reduce the heat and simmer for 15 to 20 minutes.

6. While the curry is simmering, place the Cauliflower Rice and the water in a large microwave-safe bowl. Cover the bowl with a paper towel and microwave on high for 2 minutes to steam.

7. Plate the rice and serve the curry over the top. Garnish with Thai chili peppers.

10 **Active hands-on time**

30 **Total time**

VARIATIONS: Proteins that cook quickly work well with this recipe, such as shrimp, scallops and chicken cut into small pieces. If you are able to get your hands on Kaffir lime leaves, store the extras in the freezer for future dishes.

QUICK SKILLET FRITTATA

Yield: 3-4 servings

This is such a fun recipe to feed to guests. The sweetness of the purple sweet potatoes accompanies the sausage so well. We make a version of this for breakfast at least once a month. It keeps well in the refrigerator and is quick to heat and eat when you're in a rush. Kids like frittatas, too. Give this recipe a go the next time you have some reluctant eaters in the morning.

1 tablespoon butter

½ cup diced onion

½ cup sliced button mushrooms

2 cups shredded purple sweet potatoes

½ pound kielbasa sausage, thinly sliced

12 large eggs, whisked

NOTE: Can't find your skillet lid? Cover skillet with aluminum foil in step 6.

1. In a medium-size nonstick skillet, heat the butter and sauté the onions and mushrooms for 3 minutes. Remove to a plate and set aside.

2. Place the shredded sweet potatoes on a paper plate and microwave on high for 2 minutes to soften.

3. Cook the sausage in the skillet used for the onions over medium heat until browned, about 5 minutes. Remove to a plate and set aside.

4. Cover the entire bottom of the skillet with the shredded sweet potatoes and then spoon the reserved onions and mushrooms on top.

5. Pour the whisked eggs over the vegetables in the skillet and then place the sausage slices on top like you would a pizza.

6. Cover the skillet and cook the frittata for 10 to 15 minutes, or until the eggs have firmed up.

7. Slice the frittata like a pie and serve at once.

5 **Active hands-on time**

25 **Total time**

VARIATION: If you don't have access to purple sweet potatoes, any kind of sweet potato would be fine.

SALISBURY STEAK

Yield: 4 servings

The history of this dish is rather amazing. Its namesake, Dr. James Henry Salisbury, came up with the original recipe as a means to help Civil War soldiers who suffered from various stomach issues. Dr. Salisbury recognized the link between digestive problems and heart disease, tuberculosis and psychosis. How appropriate that we bring you our version of this recipe, in hopes of ridding you of those inflammatory issues in your belly, too. The optional almond meal is used if you really like the "breading" texture of Salisbury steak. Experiment with and without it and go with what tastes best to you. Enjoy!

2 cups beef broth

2 teaspoons coconut aminos

2 teaspoons Worcestershire sauce

1 teaspoon hot sauce

1 teaspoon dried oregano

½ teaspoon freshly ground black pepper

¼ teaspoon garlic powder

1 large egg

¼ cup almond meal (optional)

1 pound ground beef

1 tablespoon ghee, plus 1 tablespoon for sautéing

2 cups thinly sliced button or cremini mushrooms

1 medium yellow onion, peeled and sliced

¼ cup unsweetened coconut milk

1. Bring the beef broth, coconut aminos, Worcestershire sauce, hot sauce, oregano, pepper and garlic powder to a boil in a medium saucepan over medium-high heat, and then reduce the heat and simmer.

2. Mix together the egg, almond meal and beef in a medium bowl, combining well. Form into oval-shaped patties about ½-inch thick.

3. In a large skillet, heat 1 tablespoon of the ghee over medium heat and brown the patties for about 90 seconds on each side. Remove to a plate.

4. Melt the remaining 1 tablespoon ghee in the skillet and sauté the mushrooms and onions until slightly caramelized, about 4 to 5 minutes.

5. Place the patties back in the skillet and spoon the onions and mushrooms on top.

6. Pour the sauce over the patties, cover and simmer for 10 minutes.

10 **Active hands-on time**

30 **Total time**

Salisbury Steak with Roasted Mashed Parsnips (page 208)

7. Add the coconut milk with a few minutes to go in the simmering to give the sauce a nice creamy texture.

8. Place the Salisbury steak on individual plates and spoon the sauce, mushrooms and onions on top. Serve at once.

SEARED SCALLOPS WITH ONION-MUSHROOM SAUCE

Yield: 4 servings

Scallops are one of Julie's most favorite foods. Can you blame her? They are a perfect combination of elegance and quick preparation. Most folks tend to overcook scallops. The secret to getting them just right is using dry high-quality scallops and getting your pan superhot. We like using coconut oil with this recipe so we can get the pan just a bit hotter before it begins to smoke. This recipe makes a fantastic appetizer for larger groups. Simply reduce the serving size down to one or two scallops per person and enjoy. — *CHARLES*

2 tablespoons ghee, plus 2 tablespoons for the sauce

2 cups sliced mushrooms (button, cremini, oyster or any assortment of your choice)

1 cup pearl onions, root ends trimmed, peeled and cut in half

12 large scallops (about 1–1½ pounds)

Salt and freshly ground black pepper, to taste

1 tablespoon coconut oil

½ cup water

Juice of 1 lemon

1 tablespoon coconut aminos

¼ teaspoon curry powder

NOTE: Be sure your scallops are good and dry before you cook them.

1. Melt 2 tablespoons of the ghee in a large nonstick skillet over medium-high heat. Sauté the mushrooms and onions for 8 minutes, or until slightly browned. Remove from the heat and cover to keep warm.

2. Heat another large skillet over high heat so that it will be hot enough for searing. Sprinkle the scallops with a little salt and pepper.

3. Add the coconut oil to the hot skillet and cook the scallops until the edges are browned, about 2 minutes per side. Remove the scallops to a large plate and cover to keep warm.

4. Add the water, lemon juice, coconut aminos and curry powder to the skillet in which the scallops were seared. Deglaze the pan with a wooden spoon while bringing the mixture to a boil and then boil for about 2 minutes.

5. Remove the sauce from the heat, and add the remaining 2 tablespoons ghee, 1 tablespoon at a time, and whisk to combine.

6. Arrange the scallops, mushrooms and onions on 4 plates and spoon the sauce over each.

5 **Active hands-on time**

20 **Total time**

STUFFED FLOUNDER

Yield: 6-8 servings

It is hard to beat a good flounder fillet. I spent many a summer in Mobile, Alabama, as a child and have very fond memories of gigging flounder with my grandfather. Point Clear, Alabama, is home to one of Mother Nature's true phenomenons, the jubilee. During a jubilee, a vast number of flounder, crabs, shrimp and other sea creatures will abandon deeper waters and will crowd together in the shallows, driven in by a depletion of oxygen in Mobile Bay. There were mornings I would awaken to Papa warming up the lantern and cinching up the burlap sack. We would walk the shallows until the sun came up and come home with a bagful of these tasty fish.

A good money-saving tip is to buy flounder whole. They are really easy to clean and you'll save quite a bit buying the entire fish (but, of course, it's a little bit time-consuming, so if you are tight on time, just buy the fillets). Stuffing the flounder fillets with crabmeat makes for a low country combination that is sure to put a grin on your face. — *CHARLES*

Olive oil, for greasing the sheet pan

2 tablespoons ghee, plus 2 tablespoons for the sauce

½ cup minced green onion

1 clove garlic, peeled and minced

1 pound lump crabmeat

Zest of 1 lemon

¼ teaspoon freshly ground black pepper

1 tablespoon chopped fresh parsley

2 pounds flounder fillets

1 cup chicken stock

Juice of 1 lemon

1 tablespoon capers

15 **Active hands-on time**

30 **Total time**

1. Preheat the oven to 350°F and grease a sheet pan with olive oil.

2. In a medium saucepan, heat 2 tablespoons of the ghee over medium heat and sauté the green onions and garlic for about 1 minute.

3. Add the crabmeat, lemon zest and pepper and cook for another 3 minutes.

4. Remove the crabmeat stuffing from the heat and stir in the parsley.

5. Cut the flounder fillets into halves or thirds, depending on the size. Place them on the sheet pan and spoon about ¼ cup crabmeat stuffing onto each fillet.

6. Fold the fillets over and arrange with the flap side facing down. Bake the fillets for 10 to 15 minutes or until cooked through.

7. While the fillets are baking, brown the remaining 2 tablespoons ghee over medium heat in the saucepan used to make the stuffing.

8. Add the chicken stock, lemon juice and capers. Bring to a quick boil, reduce the heat and simmer until the sauce thickens to a desired consistency.

9. Remove the fillets from the oven and allow to rest for 5 minutes. Arrange the fillets on plates, spoon the sauce over each and serve at once.

SOUTHWESTERN SHEPHERD'S PIE

Yield: 6–8 servings

Truth be told, we love shepherd's pie in all forms—whether it's made with ground beef, ground lamb or any other ground meat. Topping the pie with mashed cauliflower—like we did with our Farmer's "Pie" in *Paleo Comfort Foods*—was a no-brainer. This iteration ranks up there as one of our favorites, given the combination of sweet, smoky and spicy flavors from the mashed sweet potatoes and the Southwestern kick in the meat mixture. The great thing about this dish is that it freezes well and is perfect for leftovers!

FOR THE SWEET POTATOES:

2 pounds sweet potatoes, peeled and diced

1 clove garlic, peeled and crushed

½ cup unsweetened coconut milk

¼ cup to ½ cup chicken stock

1 teaspoon minced canned chipotle peppers in adobo sauce (more if you like it hotter)

Salt and freshly ground black pepper, to taste

FOR THE FILLING:

1 tablespoon oil or cooking fat of choice

2 pounds ground chicken or turkey

1 medium yellow onion, peeled and diced

4 cups frozen sliced peppers (fire-roasted is great or use fresh if you prefer)

4 cloves garlic, peeled and minced

One 14-ounce can diced fire-roasted tomatoes

2 tablespoons tomato paste

1 tablespoon ground cumin

2 teaspoons chipotle powder

1 teaspoon cayenne pepper

Salt and freshly ground black pepper, to taste

20 **Active hands-on time**

30 **Total time**

1. Preheat the oven to 350°F.

2. Prepare the sweet potatoes. Fill a medium-size pot with a few inches of water, and place a steamer basket inside. Add the sweet potatoes and garlic to the basket, and bring the water to a boil over medium-high heat. Once it boils, reduce the heat to medium, cover and cook the potatoes until they are soft, about 12 minutes.

3. Pour the potatoes and garlic into a large bowl, and add the coconut milk, some of the chicken stock, and the chipotles. Using a hand potato masher, an immersion blender or a hand mixer, mash the potatoes to the desired consistency, adding in more chicken stock as needed. Season with salt and pepper, if desired.

NOTES: If you are sensitive to the coconut flavor of coconut milk, feel free to decrease the amount of coconut milk used and increase the amount of chicken stock to your desired taste. Or, if you eat dairy, use some butter or heavy whipping cream in place of the coconut milk. If you have leftover chipotle Mashed Sweet Potatoes (194), feel free to use those.

4. While the sweet potatoes are cooking, prepare the filling by heating the oil over medium heat in a large skillet. Add the ground meat and cook until browned, about 6 to 8 minutes. Remove the meat to a large plate or bowl, reserving the oil in the pan.

5. Add the onions to the skillet in which the meat was cooked and sauté until softened. Add the peppers and garlic and sauté for 2 to 3 minutes. Mix in the tomatoes, tomato paste, cumin, chipotle powder, cayenne pepper, and salt and pepper and then stir in the reserved meat. Stir well and cook the meat filling until just heated through.

6. Divide the meat filling among 8 ramekins (about 1½- to 2-cup size) and top with the mashed sweet potatoes. Bake in the oven for 5 to 10 minutes, or until the shepherd's pie is slightly bubbly.

THANKSGIVING BURGERS

Yield: 6-8 burgers

One might call this a deconstruction—or, better yet, a reconstruction—of Thanksgiving dinner. You'll be looking around the table for cranberry sauce when you bite into this delicious burger. We think the savory succulence of the holiday season should be enjoyed all year. Consider this your invitation to celebrate your blessings any day you wish.

1 tablespoon ghee or coconut oil

½ cup minced celery

½ cup finely diced onion

½ cup finely diced button mushrooms

¼ cup chicken stock, steaming hot

½ teaspoon poultry seasoning

½ teaspoon freshly ground black pepper

¼ teaspoon salt

1 pound ground pork sausage

1 pound ground turkey

½ cup finely diced peeled Granny Smith apple (about ½ medium apple)

¼ cup minced fresh parsley

1 large egg

1. Preheat the grill to medium-high heat.

2. Melt the ghee over medium heat in a medium-size skillet and sauté the celery, onions and mushrooms for about 4 minutes, or until soft.

3. Add the chicken stock, poultry seasoning, pepper and salt. Remove from the heat and stir, combining well.

4. Transfer the vegetable mixture to a large bowl and allow to cool.

5. Add the pork, turkey, apples, parsley and egg to the vegetable mixture and mix well. Form into patties of equal size.

6. Grill the patties for about 6 minutes per side, or until cooked through.

10 **Active hands-on time**

25 **Total time**

VEGETABLE MEATZA

Yield: 6–8 servings

We got a pretty big laugh out of the fact that our first book, *Paleo Comfort Foods,* somehow ended up in the vegetarian-vegan section of some bookstores. This despite having a fried chicken recipe on the cover. Perhaps this recipe should have graced the cover of this book for good measure. This dish is really hard to mess up. Be sure to drain off the liquid from your pan before you adorn the meat "crust" with your other ingredients. We like to get ultra carnivorous and throw some sausage or bacon on top, along with the veggies. The options for what goes on top are limitless. . . . Have fun adding your own spin with the toppings.

1 teaspoon olive oil

2 pounds ground beef

1 large egg

1 tablespoon arrowroot powder

2 teaspoons onion powder

2 teaspoons dried oregano

1 teaspoon dried thyme

1 teaspoon garlic powder

One 16-ounce can diced tomatoes

One 8-ounce can tomato paste

4 cloves garlic, peeled and minced

½ cup thinly sliced button or baby bello mushrooms

½ cup roughly sliced onion

½ cup thinly sliced green bell pepper

½ cup pitted black olives, sliced

Salt and freshly ground black pepper, to taste

Minced fresh cilantro, for garnish

1. Preheat the oven to 350°F. Coat a sheet pan with the olive oil.

2. Combine the beef, egg, arrowroot powder, onion powder, oregano, thyme and garlic powder in a large bowl and mix thoroughly.

3. Roll the beef mixture out on the prepared sheet pan to ½-inch thickness. Be sure the thickness is consistent.

4. Bake the beef for 10 to 15 minutes, or until it is cooked through.

5. While the beef is baking, combine the diced tomatoes and tomato paste in a medium bowl.

6. Remove the beef "crust" from the oven and drain off the liquid.

7. Cover the "crust" with the tomato sauce, and then spread the garlic, mushrooms, onions, bell peppers and olives on top. Sprinkle with salt and pepper, if desired, and continue baking for another 5 minutes, or until the veggies are cooked.

8. Remove the meatza from the oven, garnish with cilantro, allow to cool a bit and serve.

15 **Active hands-on time**

30 **Total time**

NOTE: A rolling pin comes in handy for rolling out your meat.

SMOTHERED PORK CHOPS

Yield: 6 servings

For some reason the word *smothered* implies Southern cooking, and we're okay with that. Smothering a nice piece of pork or steak with a simple pan sauce is a way to make sure none of that tasty pan "frond" (the browned bits from a piece of meat) goes to waste. These simple smothered pork chops are quick and flavorful, and pair exceptionally well with a host of side dishes, like Chipotle Mashed Sweet Potatoes (see recipe page 194), Roasted Mashed Parsnips (see recipe page 208) or Garlicky Buttered Cabbage Noodles (see recipe page 198).

6 bone-in or boneless pork chops of desired thickness (we suggest at least 4 to 6 ounces if boneless and about 8 ounces if bone-in)

½ cup almond flour

2 tablespoons coconut flour

1 tablespoon garlic powder

1 tablespoon onion powder

1 teaspoon salt

½ teaspoon chipotle powder or cayenne pepper

¼ teaspoon smoked paprika

¼ teaspoon freshly ground black pepper

2 tablespoons oil or cooking fat of choice

2 yellow onions, peeled and thinly sliced

1 cup chicken stock

½ cup unsweetened coconut milk

1. Rinse the pork chops under cold water and pat dry.

2. Mix together the almond flour, coconut flour, garlic powder, onion powder, salt, chipotle powder, paprika and pepper in a small bowl and then pour onto a large plate. Dredge the chops in the flour mixture, shaking off the excess, and place on a clean plate. Reserve the remaining flour mixture.

3. Heat the oil in a large skillet over medium-high heat. Once the oil is barely smoking, add the pork chops and cook for 3 to 4 minutes per side, or until golden brown. Remove the chops from the skillet and set aside. (You may need to cook the pork chops in batches, depending on the size of your skillet.)

4. Add the onions to the skillet used to cook the pork chops and deglaze (stir to loosen up any browned bits) over medium heat. Cook until the onions are well browned, about 10 minutes.

5. Sprinkle the remaining flour mixture over the onions, add the chicken stock and whisk to combine. Simmer for about 5 minutes, allowing the sauce to thicken a bit, and then stir in the coconut milk.

6. Place the pork chops back into the skillet, spooning the onion sauce over them. Allow them to simmer for 5 to 7 minutes, or until the pork is cooked through.

10 **Active hands-on time**

30 **Total time**

Smothered Pork Chops with Summer Squash Sauté (page 220)
and Chipotle Mashed Sweet Potatoes (page 194)

NOTE: If you are avoiding nut flours, simply use more of the coconut flour instead of the almond flour.

BAKED EGGS WITH VEGETABLES

Yield: 2–3 servings

This is a super-quick breakfast dish and a great way to sneak in some extra vitamins, courtesy of the spinach. Should you have a tomato sauce on hand you prefer (as opposed to canned tomatoes), that would work exceptionally well as an alternative. Of course, if you wish to use more eggs in this dish, feel free!

2 tablespoons oil or cooking fat of choice

2 cups chopped button mushrooms

1 small onion, peeled and chopped

5 cups fresh spinach, washed

One 14½-ounce can crushed
  or diced tomatoes, drained
  (approximately 2 cups)

Small pinch of crushed red pepper flakes

6 large eggs

Salt and freshly ground black pepper,
  to taste

1. Heat the oil over medium heat in a large skillet that is already hot. Stir in the mushrooms and onions and cook until the onions are translucent, about 6 minutes.

2. Stir in the spinach and cook until it is bright green and barely wilted.

3. Add the tomatoes and red pepper flakes, stirring to combine.

4. When tomato-spinach mixture is heated through, create small indentations in it for the eggs. Carefully crack one egg into each of the holes, cover and cook for about 5 minutes, or until eggs achieve desired doneness.

5. Remove the baked eggs from the heat and let rest for about 3 to 4 minutes before serving. Season with salt and pepper.

10 **Active hands-on time**

15 **Total time**

VARIATIONS: If you eat dairy, adding some freshly grated Parmesan cheese or some goat cheese would be particularly tasty! This dish would be delicious with some zucchini, squash or peppers—your choice!—in addition to the spinach, onions and mushrooms.

Eggs Benedict Florentine with Hollandaise Sauce (page 202)

EGGS BENEDICT FLORENTINE

Yield: 2 servings

Ah, eggs Benedict and the often challenging poached egg. I remember back in my days of waiting tables I brought countless plates back to the line cooks, telling them that the guest was irate that their egg yolk was hard as a rock and, therefore, in their opinion, inedible. There are so many methods for poaching eggs, and it does take a little finesse, but with some practice we're confident you'll be a pro at this! The method we describe here is the one that seems to work best for us. If you have a preferred method you use, feel free! Or maybe you have one of those fancy egg poachers, in which case, now is the time to crack it out! — *JULIE*

---

2 teaspoons oil or cooking fat of choice

½ cup sliced onions

4 cups fresh spinach

2 teaspoons minced garlic

¼ teaspoon ground nutmeg

4 slices Canadian bacon (or 8 bacon strips)

4 large eggs (the freshest you can find!)

2 tablespoons white vinegar

Hollandaise Sauce (see recipe page 202)

Minced fresh chives, for garnish

Paprika or cayenne pepper, for garnish

VARIATIONS: There are plenty of variations you can try here. You can pass on the spinach or add sliced tomato, or you can just have poached eggs with the hollandaise—whatever suits you! If poached eggs don't work for you, go ahead and make this recipe with fried eggs. It will still be incredibly tasty.

20 **Active hands-on time**

30 **Total time**

1. Heat the oil over medium heat in a medium-size skillet that is already hot. Add the onions and sauté until just translucent, about 4 minutes. Add the spinach, garlic and nutmeg, mix well, and cook until the spinach is wilted and bright green. Remove the spinach mixture to a large plate and cover to keep warm.

2. To the skillet in which you cooked the spinach, add the Canadian bacon and cook over medium heat until heated through. Cover and keep warm.

3. Fill a large saucepan with 2 to 3 inches of water, place over medium-high heat, and heat to just under a simmer (160°F to 170°F). If your water starts boiling, simply reduce the heat. You'll want to see bubbles on the bottom of the saucepan, maybe one or two coming to the surface every now and then, but you don't want the water to boil.

4. Meanwhile, crack the eggs into separate small bowls or ramekins.

5. Once the water is hot, stir in the vinegar. Using a spatula or whisk, stir the hot water to make a sort of vortex in the middle of the saucepan. Gently submerge one edge of a bowl containing 1 egg in the center of the vortex of hot water and carefully let the egg slide out. Using the spatula or a spoon, push some of the egg whites inward to contain things, if necessary. Cook for approximately 3 to 4 minutes and then remove with a slotted spoon to a plate lined with paper towels.

Repeat the process with each of the eggs. To reheat the eggs, simply submerge back in the hot water for a minute before serving.

6. To assemble, place 2 pieces of Canadian bacon on each of 2 plates and top with some of the spinach. Place 1 poached egg on top of each bed of spinach, and then spoon the Hollandaise Sauce over the top. Garnish with fresh chives and paprika or cayenne pepper, if desired, and serve at once.

CHICKEN AND BROCCOLI CASSEROLE

Yield: 6–8 servings

Here in the South, we seem to have a reputation for casseroles that involve pouring a can of "cream of something" soup over some protein and vegetables, baking it for a while, and calling it a day. There's something about casseroles that make them a quintessential comfort food; they are perfect for bringing to a friend's house to welcome that new arrival or for just having on hand in the freezer. This casserole incorporates that very notion of comfort and that familiar "cream of" flavor, but without the processed foods. It's healthy and yet still incredibly filling and comforting.

2 tablespoons oil or cooking fat of choice

2 pounds boneless, skinless chicken (breast or thigh), chopped into bite-size pieces

1 medium yellow onion, peeled and diced

4 cloves garlic, peeled and minced

6 cups broccoli florets

5 cups cauliflower florets

1 cup unsweetened coconut milk

1 cup chicken stock, plus up to 1 cup extra

2 teaspoons garlic powder

2 teaspoons curry powder

½ teaspoon cayenne pepper

Salt and freshly ground black pepper, to taste

½ teaspoon paprika

10 **Active hands-on time**

30 **Total time**

1. Preheat the oven to 425°F.

2. Heat the oil over medium heat in a large skillet that is already hot, and sauté the chicken until just about cooked through, about 5 to 6 minutes. Remove the chicken to a clean large plate and set aside.

3. In the same skillet, sauté the onions and garlic until the onions are just translucent, approximately 3 to 5 minutes. Add the broccoli and about a ½ inch of water, and cook broccoli, stirring occasionally, for approximately 3 to 5 minutes, or until it is bright green.

4. Meanwhile, in a large saucepan, combine the cauliflower, coconut milk and 1 cup of the chicken stock, bring to a boil over high heat, and then reduce the heat to medium and cover. Simmer for approximately 10 minutes, or until the cauliflower is fork-tender.

5. With an immersion blender or in food processor, puree the cauliflower and the cooking liquid until no lumps remain. Add more chicken stock, if necessary, to reach the desired consistency (we prefer ours a little on the thicker side). Mix in the garlic powder, curry powder, cayenne pepper and salt and pepper.

6. Place the broccoli-onion mixture and the chicken in a 9 x 13-inch casserole dish or similar-size ovenproof dish. Stir in the cauliflower mixture and combine well. Sprinkle the top with paprika, and bake in the oven for 10 minutes, or until slightly browned on top and bubbly around the edges.

NOTES: Use cooked chicken and already made mashed cauliflower, or steam your broccoli in the microwave to save time. To freeze, follow all the steps as directed but do not bake in the oven. Instead place a layer of plastic wrap over the top of the casserole and then cover the entire dish with aluminum foil. Place in the refrigerator to cool, and once cool, move to the freezer. This casserole can remain in the freezer for several weeks. When ready to bake, thaw the casserole in the refrigerator a day or two ahead of time, and then bake in the oven for 20 to 30 minutes, or until hot throughout.

VARIATIONS: Instead of broccoli, try this dish with asparagus, or feel free to add a little sautéed spinach for some extra vitamins. Mushrooms are also incredibly tasty in this dish!

CHICKEN SALTIMBOCCA

Yield: 4 servings

Translated from Italian, *saltimbocca* means "jump in the mouth," and this recipe delivers on that promise! Though saltimbocca is most frequently associated with veal, chicken makes a fine substitute if veal isn't readily available. The key to this recipe is to make sure your chicken pieces are all of a uniform size and thickness to ensure even cooking.

4 boneless, skinless chicken breasts, pounded thin

Salt and freshly ground black pepper, to taste

8 to 12 fresh sage leaves

8 pieces very thinly sliced prosciutto

4 to 8 wooden toothpicks (optional)

2 tablespoons oil or cooking fat of choice

¾ cup chicken stock

¼ cup freshly squeezed lemon juice

1 tablespoon coconut flour (optional)

Capers and lemon pinwheels, for garnish (optional)

NOTES: Place the package of prosciutto in the freezer to make peeling off pieces much easier. A do-ahead tip: have your chicken breasts already covered with sage and prosciutto and in the refrigerator.

1. Preheat the oven to 250°F.

2. Sprinkle the chicken breasts with a little bit of salt and pepper (the prosciutto is pretty salty, so err on the side of too little salt to start). Place 2 to 3 sage leaves on top of the smooth side of each breast and wrap in 2 pieces of prosciutto (angling so as to cover the entire breast). Secure the prosciutto with toothpicks, if desired.

3. Heat the oil over medium-high heat in a large stainless-steel skillet that is already hot, then add the chicken, sage side down, and cook for 4 to 5 minutes. Flip each breast over and continuing to cook for about 3 minutes, or until the chicken is cooked through. Remove the chicken to an oven-safe plate and keep warm in the oven while you prepare the sauce.

4. Add the chicken stock and lemon juice to the skillet in which the chicken was cooked and simmer over medium heat, stirring with a whisk to scrape up the browned bits from the bottom of the pan. Whisk in the coconut flour if you prefer your sauce to be a bit creamy. Once the sauce is hot, spoon it over the chicken and serve at once. Garnish with capers and lemon pinwheels, if desired.

10 **Active hands-on time**

15 **Total time**

CHICKEN WITH MUSTARD SAUCE

Yield: 4-6 servings

When people embark on a Paleo journey, they often state that they get bored with plain old grilled chicken. A great way to change things up is by serving grilled chicken with a sauce that alters the entire flavor profile of the meat. Here's one of our favorites to try.

1 to 1½ pounds boneless, skinless chicken breasts

2 teaspoons minced fresh thyme

1 teaspoon dried tarragon

Salt and freshly ground black pepper, to taste

1 tablespoon oil or cooking fat of choice, plus 1 tablespoon for sauce

1 to 2 small shallots, peeled and minced

¼ cup chicken stock

2 tablespoons Dijon mustard

1 tablespoon red wine vinegar

1. Season the chicken breasts with thyme, tarragon, salt and pepper.

2. Heat 1 tablespoon of the oil over medium-high heat in a large skillet that is already hot. Add the chicken breasts and cook for 4 to 5 minutes per side, or until the chicken is cooked through and has browned. Remove to a large plate and keep warm.

3. To the skillet add the remaining 1 tablespoon oil and the shallots and stir, scraping up any browned bits left by the chicken. Stir in the chicken stock, mustard and vinegar, combining well.

4. Serve the chicken topped with the mustard sauce.

10 **Active hands-on time**

20 **Total time**

VARIATIONS: If you prefer a creamy mustard sauce, add about a ½ cup of coconut milk in step 3.

Chicken with Mustard Sauce with Sesame Asparagus (page 178)

CREAMY SHRIMP FRA DIAVOLO

Yield: 3–4 servings

Translated from Italian, *fra diavolo* means "brother devil." Not sure why the "brother" part, but for certain the "devil" part has to do with the spicy kick this dish has. The creaminess of the coconut milk tones down the kick just a tiny bit, so if it's not enough heat for you, feel free to add some more red pepper flakes.

1 pound extra-large shrimp (16- to 20-count), peeled and deveined

2 teaspoons crushed red pepper flakes

Pinch of salt and freshly ground black pepper

2 tablespoons olive oil or other cooking oil of choice

1 medium yellow onion, peeled and sliced

5 cloves garlic, peeled and minced

One 14½-ounce can diced or crushed tomatoes (San Marzano or home canned are best!)

½ cup dry white wine (optional)

½ cup unsweetened coconut milk

1 tablespoon minced fresh basil

1. In a medium bowl, combine the shrimp, red pepper flakes and salt and pepper.

2. Heat the oil over medium-high heat in a large skillet that is already hot. Add the shrimp (being careful not to overcrowd the skillet) and sauté for about 2 to 3 minutes, or until just barely cooked through. If the skillet will be overcrowded, cook the shrimp in two batches. With tongs or a slotted spoon, remove the shrimp to a clean plate and set aside.

3. Add the onions and garlic to the skillet in which the shrimp were cooked, and sauté, stirring, until the onions are translucent, about 4 to 5 minutes. Stir in the tomatoes with their juices, wine and coconut milk, and then reduce the heat to medium and cook for about 10 minutes, or until the sauce thickens slightly.

4. Add the shrimp (and any accumulated shrimp juices) and the basil to the skillet and stir to blend all the flavors together.

5. Remove the shrimp from the heat and serve at once.

10 **Active hands-on time**

20 **Total time**

VARIATIONS: While this recipe calls for shrimp, you could easily use scallops, chicken or pretty much any other protein of your choosing. If you don't feel like a creamy dish (or you are averse to coconut), simply leave the coconut milk out.

GINGER-GARLIC-SCALLION-CRUSTED CHICKEN

Yield: 6-8 servings

Back in 1997 or so, when I was waiting tables at the Druid Hills Golf Club in Atlanta, my friend Jonn "Nish" Nishiyama won best seafood chef in Georgia for his ginger-garlic-scallion-crusted halibut. It was the one dish that we could not remove from the formal dining room menu at the golf club—everyone absolutely loved this dish (myself included). Ever since then, coating things in a ginger, garlic and scallion paste has been a go-to technique of mine, and I have Nish to thank for the inspiration. Not only does the crust taste great, but it also adds some great color to the dish. — *JULIE*

---

2 pounds boneless, skinless chicken breasts

½ cup coarsely chopped scallions

2- to 3-inch piece of fresh ginger, peeled

4 cloves garlic, peeled

Salt and freshly ground black pepper, to taste

2 tablespoons olive oil

1 tablespoon oil or cooking fat of choice

½ cup almonds, coarsely chopped

1. Preheat the oven to 450°F.

2. Cover the chicken breasts with plastic wrap on both sides and, using a meat mallet, pound them to an even thickness, about ½ to ¾ inch thick.

3. Combine the scallions, ginger, garlic, salt and pepper in a food processor or blender. Pulse a few times to combine. Add the 2 tablespoons olive oil to the food processor and process into a paste.

4. Heat the 1 tablespoon oil over medium-high heat in a large ovenproof skillet and place the chicken in the skillet, smooth side down. Sear the chicken for about 2 to 3 minutes on one side, or until lightly browned and the chicken easily releases from the pan.

5. Flip the chicken breasts and turn off the burner. Coat the seared side with the ginger-garlic-scallion paste and sprinkle the nuts on top, pressing on them so they adhere to the paste.

10 **Active hands-on time**

25 **Total time**

6. Place the chicken in the oven for 10 minutes, or until it is cooked through (internal temperature reaches at least 170°F) and the nut crust on the top is golden brown.

7. Allow the chicken to rest for 5 minutes and serve.

NOTES: The ginger-garlic-scallion crust is also incredibly tasty on fish. The crust also works well with macadamia nuts instead of almonds. If you're feeling decadent and you eat butter, you can make a beurre blanc sauce (using coconut milk as a substitute for cream) and serve this chicken with some of that.

LAMB CHOPS WITH FIGS AND OLIVES

Yield: 6–8 servings

The salty-sweet combination of briny olives with sweet figs tastes great with these lamb chops. If lamb isn't available, try this with pork chops.

FOR THE FIG AND OLIVE MIXTURE:

1 cup dried figs, stems removed

1 cup boiling water

¾ cup mix of green and kalamata olives, plus ¼ cup for garnish

3 tablespoons olive oil

2 tablespoons pine nuts

1 tablespoon balsamic vinegar

1 clove garlic, peeled

1 teaspoon minced fresh rosemary

FOR THE LAMB CHOPS:

2 pounds lamb chops

Salt and freshly ground black pepper, to taste

NOTES: Black Mission figs are preferred here. If you can't find them, use any figs you can get your hands on. If you have fresh figs in season where you are, chop some up to serve alongside this dish.

1. Heat a grill pan over medium-high heat or heat up your outdoor grill.

2. Meanwhile prepare the fig and olive mixture. Place the figs in a medium-size bowl, add the boiling water and soak for 10 to 15 minutes. Drain well.

3. Combine ¾ cup of the olives, the olive oil, pine nuts, vinegar, garlic and rosemary in a food processor and process until smooth.

4. Season the lamb chops with salt and pepper. Once your grill pan or grill is hot, grill the chops for 3 to 4 minutes per side, cooking them longer or shorter depending upon your desired doneness.

5. Slice the remaining ¼ cup olives. Serve the chops with the fig and olive mixture, and garnish with the sliced olives.

15 **Active hands-on time**

25 **Total time**

LIME AND COCONUT CHICKEN "RICE"

Yield: 3-4 servings

This recipe is a bit like fried rice, but with a tropical flair. Personally, we love coconut, so if we could live somewhere tropical and have a coconut tree farm, we'd be in hog heaven. If coconut isn't your thing, you could create this dish with some chicken stock in place of the coconut milk. Your rice won't be as creamy, but the lime will still add great flavor.

1 tablespoon oil or cooking fat of choice

1 pound boneless, skinless chicken breasts or thighs, cut into bite-size pieces

3 cups Cauliflower Rice (see How to Make Cauliflower Rice page 45)

1 cup unsweetened coconut milk

½ cup chicken stock

Zest and juice of 1 lime

2 tablespoons thinly sliced green onion

2 teaspoons fish sauce

1. Heat the oil over medium heat in a large skillet that is already hot. Add the chicken and sauté until cooked through, about 4 to 5 minutes.

2. Add the remaining ingredients to the skillet. Mix well, and cook until the "rice" has softened and the liquid has cooked off.

 VARIATIONS: If you don't have chicken on hand, try this with shrimp or pork instead.

10 **Active hands-on time**

20 **Total time**

PAN-SAUTÉED STEAKS WITH CREAMY LEEKS AND MUSHROOMS

Yield: 6–8 servings

I threw this one together one night for us with some fresh leeks from our local farmers' market. The secret to giving the leeks a robust flavor is to capitalize on the frond (browned bits) left behind by the steaks. I wish you could bottle that to always have on hand! — *JULIE*

2 pounds New York strip steaks (aka top loin), about 1½-2 inches thick

Steak seasonings of choice (salt, pepper, cumin, etc.)

2 tablespoons oil or cooking fat of choice

1½ cups beef stock

1 cup thinly sliced leeks (white and light green parts)

1 cup unsweetened coconut milk

1 ounce porcini mushrooms, chopped and soaked in ½ cup boiling hot water for 10 minutes

2 teaspoons balsamic vinegar

Salt and freshly ground black pepper, to taste

1. Pat the steaks dry, and season with the steak seasonings of your choice.

2. Preheat a large stainless-steel skillet or cast-iron frying pan over medium heat. Add the oil, and once it's hot, add the steaks. The steaks should sizzle immediately when added to the pan.

3. Sear the steaks for approximately 3 to 4 minutes on one side and then flip over and cook for another 2 to 3 minutes (longer if you prefer your steak more well-done). Remove the steaks from the pan to a large plate and let rest.

4. Add the beef stock and leeks to the pan, and scrape up all the browned bits from the bottom. Reduce the heat to medium-low and simmer for 5 minutes.

5. Stir in the coconut milk, mushrooms, the mushroom soaking water, balsamic vinegar, salt and pepper.

6. Simmer over medium-low heat until the sauce has thickened somewhat, about 5 to 7 minutes.

7. Serve the creamy leeks and mushrooms over or alongside the steaks.

10 **Active hands-on time**

25 **Total time**

VARIATIONS: If you don't have New York strip steaks on hand, use whatever cuts of steak are accessible to you. Flat iron steaks, hanger steaks and rib eyes would all be just fine.

Pan-Sautéed Steaks with Creamy Leeks and Mushrooms with Sautéed Brussels Sprouts (page 214)

PORK CHOPS WITH TROPICAL SALSA

Yield: 6-8 servings

There's something about a tropical salsa paired with a seemingly mundane seared piece of meat that makes everything taste that much better. And, fortunately, tropical salsas like this one pair perfectly with hot summer nights, making dishes like this seem even cooler than they are—not to mention the fact that the salsa is just lovely all on its own!

FOR THE PORK CHOPS:

2 pounds boneless pork chops

1 teaspoon garlic powder

1 teaspoon ground cumin

¼ teaspoon salt

¼ teaspoon freshly ground black pepper

1 tablespoon oil or fat of choice

FOR THE SALSA:

2 medium ripe mangoes, peeled, pitted and diced

⅓ cup diced red bell pepper

¼ cup finely minced fresh mint

3 tablespoons minced red onion

1 tablespoon fresh lime juice

1. Pat the pork chops dry and sprinkle both sides with the garlic powder, cumin, salt and pepper.

2. Heat the oil over medium-high heat in a large stainless-steel skillet that is already hot. When the oil is barely smoking, add the pork chops, sear for approximately 5 minutes on the first side, and then turn over and sear for 3 to 4 minutes, or until the internal temperature is 145°F. Remove the pork chops to a large plate and let rest.

3. While the pork is resting, combine all the salsa ingredients in a medium bowl. Serve the pork chops topped with the salsa.

10 **Active hands-on time**

20 **Total time**

VARIATIONS: If you can't find mangoes, feel free to substitute pineapple. This dish would also be great with chicken or fish in place of the pork.

QUICK COQ AU VIN

Yield: 6–8 servings

You may think of Julia Child when you hear the words *coq au vin*. She helped to bring this classic, comforting French dish into the hearts and stomachs of so many Americans. As I shared in *Paleo Comfort Foods,* the first time I made a coq au vin in public was for a cooking demonstration at Williams-Sonoma, and the recipe they wanted us to use called for igniting the brandy poured into the dish. Fortunately, I did not burn off my eyebrows, and even more fortunately, I created a much quicker version of the dish, one without the flambé risk to one's face. — *JULIE*

4 bacon strips

2 pounds boneless, skinless chicken thighs

¼ cup coconut or almond flour (optional)

½ teaspoon salt

½ teaspoon freshly ground black pepper

1 tablespoon oil or cooking fat of choice (if not using bacon drippings)

2 cups quartered button or cremini mushrooms

1 cup pearl onions (or 1 cup chopped yellow onion)

2 cloves garlic, peeled and minced

2 cups chicken broth

1 cup dry red wine

1 tablespoon tomato paste

2 fresh thyme sprigs

1. Heat a large Dutch oven or covered pot over medium heat. When hot, add the bacon and cook until crispy. Remove the bacon strips to a plate lined with paper towels. Reserve the bacon grease in the Dutch oven for cooking the chicken.

2. In a medium bowl, toss the chicken with the flour, salt and pepper. If not using the bacon drippings, heat the oil or cooking fat over medium heat in the same pot used for the bacon. Cook in the Dutch oven over medium heat until the chicken is browned on all sides, about 3 to 4 minutes per side. Remove to a plate.

3. Add the mushrooms, onions and garlic to the Dutch oven and cook over medium heat, stirring well, until the mushrooms are slightly softened, about 2 to 3 minutes.

4. Add the chicken broth, wine, tomato paste and thyme and mix well, making sure tomato paste gets fully integrated. Add the chicken and any juices that may have accumulated. Cover, reduce the heat to medium-low and cook for 10 to 15 minutes, or until the chicken is cooked through.

5. Break the bacon into bite-size pieces and mix into the coq au vin. Serve hot.

15 **Active hands-on time**

30 **Total time**

NOTE: We suggest doubling this recipe, as it freezes exceptionally well.

QUICK ROASTED WHOLE CHICKEN

Yield: 6-8 servings

What's that you say? It's impossible to cook a whole roast chicken in under an hour? I forget where or when I first experienced spatchcocked chicken (which is basically just chicken with the backbone removed, allowing the bird to lie flat), but it made me realize that indeed you can have a delicious roast chicken on your table in under an hour. A revelation indeed! — *JULIE*

1 pastured chicken (3 to 4 pounds), rinsed and patted dry

3 tablespoons ghee, softened

Zest of 1 lemon

3 cloves garlic, peeled and minced

2 tablespoons minced fresh flat-leaf (Italian) parsley

Salt and freshly ground black pepper, to taste

Lemon pinwheels, for serving

NOTES: This recipe makes for great leftovers. Use any remaining chicken for dishes like Creamy Cauliflower and Chicken Soup (see recipe page 56), Tortilla-less Soup (see recipe page 70) or Chicken and Broccoli Casserole (see recipe page 127). Be sure to save the chicken carcass to make your very own chicken stock!

1. Preheat the oven to 450°F.

2. To spatchcock your chicken, lay it flat on a cutting board, breast side down. Using kitchen shears, cut along both sides of the backbone to remove it. (We suggest saving the backbone for use in making your own chicken stock!) Once the backbone has been removed, flip your chicken over and press down to flatten the bird. You may hear bones cracking, and that is totally normal.

3. In a small bowl, combine the ghee, lemon zest, garlic and parsley. Carefully reach under the skin on the chicken breasts and thighs and massage in some of the ghee mixture throughout. Rub any remaining ghee mixture on the outside of the skin.

4. Sprinkle the chicken all over with salt and pepper and place in a large ovenproof skillet (12 to 14 inches in diameter) or on a broiler pan.

5. Place the chicken in the oven and roast for 35 to 40 minutes, or until the chicken thigh meat registers 165°F on a meat thermometer. Serve with lemon.

5 **Active hands-on time**

45 **Total time**

VARIATION: There are so many ways you can season the bird. Use whatever seasonings you most prefer and enjoy!

RED CURRY CHICKEN

Yield: 3-4 servings

Here's a quick and flavorful take on curried chicken tenders. While we prefer things on the hotter side, if you prefer a milder dish use less curry paste.

1 tablespoon oil or cooking fat of choice

1 pound skinless, boneless chicken breasts, cut into ½-inch strips

2 tablespoons sunflower seed butter or creamy nut butter (almond, cashew, etc.)

1 tablespoon red curry paste

2 cups unsweetened coconut milk

2 teaspoons coconut aminos

Juice of 1 lime

 VARIATIONS: You can use any kind of boneless, skinless chicken meat in this. Of course, you can also use pork or beef, if that's more to your liking. This super-easy dish invites the addition of lots of vegetables (essentially making it a traditional curry dish). Feel free to get creative! Serve the chicken over Cauliflower Rice (see How to Make Cauliflower Rice page 45), simple shredded cabbage, or kelp or yam noodles (shirataki), found in most Asian markets.

1. Heat the oil over medium heat in a large skillet that is already hot. Once your oil is just about smoking, add the chicken and cook for a few minutes on each side. The chicken should not be cooked through all the way. Remove the chicken to a clean plate and set aside.

2. To the skillet in which the chicken was cooked, add the sunflower seed butter and the curry paste, spreading the mixture around in the skillet until aromatic, but not burnt. Stir in the coconut milk, coconut aminos and lime juice, mixing well.

3. Return your chicken to the skillet and simmer for 5 to 7 minutes, or until it is cooked through and the sauce has reduced somewhat.

10-15 **Active hands-on time**

20 **Total time**

SAUTÉED STEAKS WITH TOMATO PAN SAUCE AND WILTED ARUGULA

Yield: 6–8 servings

Each year we're certain to plant a variety of cherry tomato plants in our garden, in addition to our big tomato plants, as it's just so hard to resist those bite-size bursts of sweetness. Of course, the colors—yellow, red, orange—make them that much more appealing, and they are always fun in a variety of recipes or when just adding great color to your salad.

2 pounds steaks of your choice (rib eye, porterhouse, T-bone), about 1½-2 inches thick

Salt and freshly ground black pepper

2 tablespoons oil or cooking fat of choice

2 tablespoons minced shallots

½ cup beef stock

1 pint assorted cherry tomatoes

4 cups arugula

2 tablespoons balsamic vinegar

NOTES: Be sure to check the label on your balsamic vinegar. Some aren't true balsamic vinegar, but rather vinegar with caramel coloring added.

1. Sprinkle the steaks liberally with salt and pepper.

2. Heat the oil over medium-high heat in a large cast-iron skillet or other skillet that is already hot. Add the steaks and sear for 3 to 5 minutes per side (longer if you like your steak well-done). Remove the steaks to a clean large plate and allow them to rest while you make the sauce.

3. Reduce the heat to medium and add the shallots and a few teaspoons of the beef stock to the skillet. Scrape up any of the browned bits left by the steaks. Add the tomatoes and cook for about 1 minute to slightly soften them.

4. Add the remaining stock, arugula and balsamic vinegar and cook just until the arugula is wilted.

5. Arrange the steaks on plates, place the tomatoes and arugula all around, spoon on the sauce and serve at once.

10–15 **Active hands-on time**

20 **Total time**

VARIATION: Instead of wilting the arugula, serve these steaks, with the tomatoes and sauce, over fresh arugula. They're super tasty that way, as well.

SEARED SALMON WITH QUICK PESTO MAYO

Yield: 6–8 servings

A beautiful piece of seared salmon on its own is just about as good as it gets. However, we do love serving the healthy fish with some pesto mayo, which we find takes the salmon from great to *really* great. Our advice: find the best salmon you can. Typically, you won't find much in the way of fresh wild-caught salmon in the winter months (and if you do, you're likely to pay a premium). Salmon season usually starts in February and peaks in the summertime. Sockeye, Coho and Copper River are all very tasty!

FOR THE SALMON:

2 tablespoons oil or cooking fat of choice

2 pounds wild-caught salmon fillets, skin on and cut into 4- to 6-ounce portions

Salt and freshly ground black pepper, to taste

FOR THE PESTO MAYO:

½ cup fresh basil leaves

2 tablespoons toasted pine nuts

2 cloves garlic, peeled and crushed

¼ teaspoon salt

2 tablespoons olive oil

⅓ cup Paleo Mayonnaise (see recipe page 204)

1. Heat the oil over medium-high heat in a large skillet that is already hot. Pat the salmon pieces dry with paper towels. Season with salt and pepper. Once the oil is hot, carefully add the salmon pieces to the skillet, skin side down. Press down on them with a spatula when they are first added to the pan to prevent the skin from shrinking too much. Sear the salmon for about 5 minutes, or until the skin is crispy and the fish easily releases from the pan. Carefully flip over and sear the skinless side for 1 to 2 minutes for a medium doneness. Remove to a plate and keep warm.

2. Combine the basil, pine nuts, garlic and salt in a food processor and puree. With the food processor running, slowly add the olive oil and process until smooth.

3. Transfer the pesto to a small bowl and stir in the mayo. Serve alongside the salmon. Optional: garnish with additional toasted pine nuts.

5–10 **Active hands-on time**

15 **Total time**

NOTES: If you have your own homemade basil pesto already on hand, you've just made this quicker and easier on yourself! If not, no worries. The pesto here is super quick and makes for a tasty condiment that goes beautifully with the salmon. If you prefer a thinner pesto mayo, simply add more olive oil to the mixture to thin it.

SPICY SALMON CAKES

Yield: 3-4 servings

One of our favorite pieces from the humor blog *The Oatmeal* pays homage to sriracha. We have one of their posters hanging at our gym. It features this spicy sauce with a caption that reads, "You're also good on...pretty much any animal that has passed through death and fire and wound up in my mouth." Sriracha—a chili paste—is a staple in our house, and it gives these salmon cakes a wonderful little kick! It's super easy to make your own sriracha (which enables you to omit the sugar), or you could always use chili garlic paste instead of the famous rooster bottle. Huy Fong makes a good sriracha (but it does contain sugar—about one gram of sugar per teaspoon) and a chili garlic paste (that is just like sriracha but without the sugar). More and more grocery stores now stock these popular condiments in the ethnic aisle.

1 pound canned wild-caught salmon (or equivalent amount of cooked fish)

¼ cup Paleo Mayonnaise (see recipe page 204) or store-bought mayo (just check your labels!)

1 large egg

2 tablespoons finely minced green onion (white and green parts)

2 teaspoons sriracha (or more if you like yours extra spicy!)

1 teaspoon sesame oil

1 tablespoon oil or cooking fat of choice

1. Combine all the ingredients except for the 1 tablespoon oil or cooking fat in a medium bowl. Form into fish cakes of equal size. We like ours about 2 to 3 inches in diameter.

2. Heat the oil in a large frying pan over medium heat. Working in batches, if need be, cook the salmon cakes for about 4 to 5 minutes per side, or until golden brown and hot. Alternatively, you can finish these off in a 350°F oven, should you choose, about 8 to 10 minutes.

10 **Active hands-on time**

20 **Total time**

NOTE: We have found great canned wild-caught salmon at Costco for an excellent price. Just be sure to check your labels!

STEAK BITES WITH CREAMY MUSHROOM SAUCE

Yield: 3–4 servings

This is one of those dishes where the sauce takes an ordinary dish and elevates it to the next level. While we use top sirloin here, you could use a whole flank steak, or if you'd like to transform this dish into something higher end, go for some petit filets, kept whole as medallions. Either way, you'll have a rather indulgent meal.

½ ounce dried porcini mushrooms

2 cups boiling water

1 tablespoon oil or cooking fat of choice

1 pound top sirloin steak, cut into 1-inch pieces

2 tablespoons finely minced shallots

2 cups sliced baby bella or cremini mushrooms

2 cloves garlic, peeled and minced

¼ teaspoon sea salt

¼ teaspoon freshly ground black pepper

½ cup red wine (like pinot noir) or beef stock

2 tablespoons unsweetened coconut milk

1 tablespoon minced fresh thyme

NOTES: As a time-saver, buy presliced, prewashed mushrooms.

1. Place the porcini mushrooms in a small bowl and pour the boiling water over them. Allow them to sit for 15 minutes. After soaking, strain the mushrooms through a sieve over a bowl, reserving all the soaking liquid.

2. Meanwhile, heat the oil over medium heat in a large skillet that is already hot. Once the oil is hot, add the pieces of steak and sear for a few minutes on each side, or until they are medium rare. Using tongs, remove the steak bites to a plate and tent with aluminum foil to keep warm. Reserve any fat in the pan.

3. Add the shallots to the same pan in which the steak was cooked, and sauté for about 1 minute, scraping up any of the browned bits from the bottom of the pan.

4. Add the baby bella or cremini mushrooms to the pan and sauté for about 3 minutes, or until the mushrooms just start to soften. Add the garlic, the reserved porcinis, salt and pepper, and stir to combine.

5. Pour in the wine (or stock) and cook until the liquid has almost evaporated. Stir in the reserved porcini soaking liquid, coconut milk and thyme, and cook for about 5 minutes, or until slightly thickened.

6. Serve the steak bites topped with the mushroom sauce. Feel free to serve extra sauce on the side!

10 **Active hands-on time**

30 **Total time**

VARIATIONS: This mushroom sauce goes great with chicken, as well.

Steak Bites with Creamy Mushroom Sauce with Sautéed Kale with a Kick (page 216)

STUFFED PORK CHOPS

Yield: 4-6 servings

This recipe was inspired by some thick, fresh, incredible pork chops we got from Pine Street Market here in Atlanta (and they in turn get all their pork from Gum Creek Farms, a local farm raising pigs right). We weren't sure what to do with them but wanted dinner on the table relatively quickly, so I threw together this stuffing and, voilà, off we went. Charles wasn't too unhappy with the results, either! — *JULIE*

4 boneless pork chops (6 to 8 ounces each), ¾ to 1 inch thick

1 tablespoon oil or cooking fat of choice, plus 1 tablespoon for cooking chops

½ cup minced onion

1 cup minced fresh button or cremini mushrooms

½ cup diced Granny Smith apple (about ½ medium apple)

1 clove garlic, peeled and minced

1 teaspoon crushed dried sage

½ teaspoon ground rosemary

8 wooden toothpicks

Salt and freshly ground black pepper, to taste

NOTE: This is one of those times when a Slap Chop comes in really handy to finely chop up those mushrooms and onions.

1. Cut a pocket in a pork chop by inserting a knife tip into the side of your chop and, without cutting through to the other side, moving your knife back and forth to within ½ inch or so of the chop's edges. You want to keep the knife opening small to help keep the stuffing intact. Repeat for the remaining chops.

2. Heat 1 tablespoon of the oil over medium heat in a large stainless-steel skillet that is already hot. Stir in the onions and sauté for 1 to 2 minutes. Add the mushrooms, apples and garlic and sauté until softened, about 4 to 6 minutes.

3. Add the sage and rosemary and mix well. Remove the stuffing mixture from the skillet to a medium bowl. Wipe the skillet clean.

4. Stuff the pork chops with the stuffing mixture, and insert toothpicks along the edge to keep the stuffing inside the chops. Sprinkle with salt and pepper.

5. Heat the remaining 1 tablespoon oil over medium-high heat in the skillet used to make the stuffing. Cook the pork chops for about 6 to 8 minutes per side, or until the internal temperature reaches at least 145°F.

15 **Active hands-on time**

30 **Total time**

VARIATIONS: If you want to make a quick sauce to serve over the chops, simply deglaze the pan you cooked the chops in by adding ½ cup to 1 cup of either chicken stock or apple juice (or cider) and then whisking to break up any of the browned bits in the pan. You can season the sauce with some herbs (like sage or rosemary), or just serve as is.

Stuffed Pork Chops with Butternut Squash Puree (page 170)

SZECHUAN STIR-FRY

Yield: 3-4 servings

Szechuan peppercorns were actually banned in the United States for almost forty years, for fear that they might spread a bacterial disease to our citrus trees. In 2005 the ban was lifted, but I'm figuring some houses might want to impose such a ban on these for their heat—they create an almost numbing sensation. It's slightly different than just being hot, and most struggle with the best way to describe it. If you can't find Szechuan peppercorns—or you are too scared to try them!—opt for red chili paste instead.

1 pound top sirloin, flank steak or beef tenderloin, cut into 2-inch strips

1 tablespoon Szechuan peppercorns, toasted and ground in a spice grinder (optional)

1 tablespoon coconut oil

2 teaspoons red chili paste (use more if you cannot find Szechuan peppercorns)

2 teaspoons minced fresh ginger

2 cloves garlic, peeled and minced

2 medium red bell peppers, seeded, deribbed and cut into strips

8-10 medium asparagus spears, cut into 2-inch pieces

¼ cup chicken stock

1 tablespoon coconut aminos

1 teaspoon sesame oil

1. Combine the beef and the ground peppercorns in a medium bowl.

2. Heat the oil over high heat in a large skillet or wok that is already hot. When the oil is hot, add beef, chili paste, ginger and garlic and cook for 1 to 2 minutes.

3. Add the peppers, asparagus, chicken stock, coconut aminos and sesame oil and stir to combine well. Cook until the beef is cooked through, about 3 to 5 minutes.

 VARIATIONS: Any protein would be delicious in this recipe—pork, chicken, seafood, etc.—as would just about any vegetable. Go with what suits your taste!

5-10 **Active hands-on time**

20 **Total time**

NOTE: This is a relatively hot and spicy dish. If you prefer things on the mild side, ditch the Szechuan peppercorns and go easy on the chili paste.

CHAPTER 5
SIDES AND SAUCES

Avocado Dipping Sauce 166

Barbecue Sauce 168

Butternut Squash Puree. 170

Pan-Fried Okra. 172

Sautéed Mushrooms. 174

Seasoned Jicama Fries 176

Sesame Asparagus 178

Sweet and Savory Roasted Cauliflower 180

Tzatziki Sauce 182

Apple-Cucumber Relish. 184

Apple and Pear Sauce 186

Bacon and Okra Pilau 188

Bagna Càuda 190

Basil Pesto 192

Chipotle Mashed Sweet Potatoes. 194

Curry Noodles 196

Garlicky Buttered Cabbage Noodles 198

Ginger-Glazed Carrots 200

Hollandaise Sauce 202

Paleo Mayonnaise and Two Aiolis 204

Peach Salsa. 206

Roasted Mashed Parsnips. 208

Root Veggie Cakes 210

Sausage and Apple Dressing 212

Sautéed Brussels Sprouts 214

Sautéed Kale with a Kick 216

Spicy Plum Sauce 218

Summer Squash Sauté. 220

AVOCADO DIPPING SAUCE

Yield: 1–1½ cups

This recipe embodies quick and easy. If you are ever in a pinch for a spread, aioli or any other kind of sauce, this is a trusted go-to. It is so simple and incredibly tasty. It's always a crowd pleaser, and it's easy to double or triple this recipe for guests and parties. This is also something great to make if you ever have avocados in the house that are about to go bad. The lime juice extends the life of the avocados a few extra days and gives you the chance to enjoy them on just about anything. Consider substituting different ingredients for the Dijon mustard to put your own spin on this.

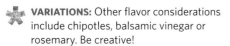

1 medium ripe Hass avocado

Juice of 1 lime

1 clove garlic, peeled

1 tablespoon Dijon mustard

½ teaspoon freshly ground black pepper

¼ teaspoon salt

2 to 4 tablespoons extra-virgin olive oil, as desired

1. Halve the avocado, and remove the pit and peel.

2. Place the avocado halves and the rest of the ingredients in a food processor or mini-blender and pulse until smooth and creamy.

3. If you want this to have a thinner consistency, stir in the olive oil to thin it out so that it is more like a dressing than a dipping sauce.

4. Serve as a spread, dip or dressing.

VARIATIONS: Other flavor considerations include chipotles, balsamic vinegar or rosemary. Be creative!

5 **Active hands-on time**

5 **Total time**

BARBECUE SAUCE

Yield: 2 cups

You have to look long and hard to find someone who doesn't like barbecue sauce. We put this sauce on everything from chicken and pork to fish or scrambled eggs. Our "quick and easy" version still packs a ton of flavor and keeps in the fridge for quite a while. Get this recipe started before you fire up the grill to ensure that it is ready by the time you need to cook. The carrot juice is optional and adds just a bit more sweetness to the overall flavor. Having a container of this handy will add a new zip to leftovers.

1 tablespoon extra-virgin olive oil

¼ cup chopped onion

3 cloves garlic, peeled and minced

One 14½-ounce can diced tomatoes

1½ cups chicken stock

½ cup carrot juice (optional)

¼ cup apple cider vinegar

2 tablespoons honey (optional)

1½ tablespoons yellow mustard

1 tablespoon Worcestershire sauce

1 tablespoon chili powder

1 teaspoon balsamic vinegar

1 teaspoon freshly ground black pepper

½ teaspoon salt

1. Heat the oil over medium heat in a medium saucepan, and then sauté the onions and garlic for about 2 minutes.

2. Add the remaining ingredients and bring to a boil. Cover, reduce the heat and simmer for 20 minutes, stirring occasionally.

3. Pour the mixture in a blender (or use an immersion blender) and puree until smooth.

NOTES: Always be careful when putting hot liquid in a blender. If you desire a thinner sauce, thin to your desired consistency with added stock or water.

5 **Active hands-on time**

30 **Total time**

Barbeque Sauce with Bacon- and Basil-Wrapped Shrimp (page 24).

BUTTERNUT SQUASH PUREE

Yield: 6-8 servings

This is an amazingly tasty side and pairs well with just about any pork dish. My inspiration for this recipe came on our last night dining out before the baby was born. I ordered porchetta, which was served over a sweet potato puree. I hope you like my version using butternut squash. Now, if we could only figure out a way to make porchetta in less than 45 minutes. — *CHARLES*

3 tablespoons ghee

½ cup finely chopped sweet onion, such as Spanish, Bermuda or Vidalia

1 clove garlic, peeled and minced

1 pound butternut squash, peeled, seeded and cubed

1 large Granny Smith apple, peeled, cored and cut into pieces

½ cup chicken stock

¼ cup unsweetened coconut milk

1 tablespoon freshly squeezed lemon juice

½ teaspoon ground cinnamon

⅛ teaspoon ground ginger

Salt and freshly ground black pepper, to taste

1. Melt the ghee in a Dutch oven over medium heat and sauté the onions for about 5 minutes, adding the garlic in the last minute.

2. Stir in the squash, reduce the heat to low and cook, covered, for another 5 minutes.

3. Add the apples, chicken stock, coconut milk, lemon juice, cinnamon, ginger, and salt and pepper; cover and simmer for 10 more minutes.

4. Uncover and cool for a few minutes.

5. Puree with an immersion blender, or transfer the squash mixture to a food processor or blender and puree in batches.

6. Season with salt and pepper, to taste, and serve.

NOTE: Buy precut butternut squash to save time.

10 **Active hands-on time**

30 **Total time**

VARIATIONS: Use your favorite apple variety instead of Granny Smith. You can also add a tablespoon of chipotle pepper to the puree for a smoky/fiery flavor.

PAN-FRIED OKRA

Yield: 4–6 servings

We love our okra in the South and it lends itself to different flavor combinations. If you want to add a little honey to the liquids for sweetness, be my guest. To lend a bit more tang to the dish, simply add some lemon zest as the okra is cooking. Don't have a wok handy? Then just use a frying pan. The okra will get a bit slimy as it cooks. You can continue cooking until it begins to caramelize, or even longer, if you prefer.

1 tablespoon coconut oil

2 teaspoons minced fresh ginger

2 cloves garlic, peeled and minced

1 pound okra, cut in half lengthwise

1 tablespoon coconut aminos

1 teaspoon freshly squeezed lemon juice

Freshly cracked pepper, to taste

NOTES: Keep the okra whole to avoid the slimy texture and to cut down on prep time.

1. Heat the coconut oil over high heat in a wok.

2. Sauté the ginger and garlic, and when the garlic begins to brown, add the okra and toss frequently for about 8 minutes.

3. Add the coconut aminos and lemon juice and cook until the liquid is nearly gone.

4. Season with freshly cracked pepper and serve.

5 **Active hands-on time**

20 **Total time**

SAUTÉED MUSHROOMS

Yield: 6-8 servings

Twice a year, I get to go mushroom hunting with my buddy Todd Mussman. We hunt morels in the spring and then go looking for chanterelles when summer rolls in. There are some rather bountiful spots for these cherished sources of flavor that are just ten minutes from our house. The hunt is quite fun but pales in comparison to the feast that comes after. We spent some time at Todd's house this past Thanksgiving. Our meat "dessert" was a truffle-infused foie gras with a mushroom reduction poured over the top. Honestly, it may be the tastiest dessert that has ever passed my lips. I can't help but think his reduction incorporated some of the bounty we gathered earlier in the year. Bring some earthy, rich flavor to any entrée with this recipe. Your taste buds will thank you. — *CHARLES*

1 tablespoon finely chopped dried porcini mushrooms

1 cup beef broth

3 tablespoons butter

1 medium shallot, peeled and thinly sliced

1 clove garlic, peeled and minced

1 pound assorted fresh mushrooms, chopped to desired size

2 teaspoons dried sage

½ teaspoon salt

Freshly ground black pepper, to taste

1. Place the porcini mushrooms in a small bowl, add the beef broth and soak porcinis.

2. Meanwhile, melt the butter in a large saucepan over medium heat, and sauté the shallots and garlic for about 2 minutes.

3. Add the fresh mushrooms and sage and cook for 8 minutes, stirring frequently.

4. Add the porcinis, broth and salt, and continue cooking until very little liquid is left.

5. Season with pepper and serve.

NOTE: Leftovers go great with eggs for breakfast.

10 **Active hands-on time***

25 **Total time**

*Not counting the time spent foraging for mushrooms!

SEASONED JICAMA FRIES

Yield: 4-6 servings

Part of the transition to a Paleo lifestyle is the repositioning of the mind and palate around certain foods. This recipe is a classic example of this. These are a fantastic treat and will go well with nearly any entrée. To fully enjoy them, you have to get over your predisposition for classic French fries. The jicama has a crispness that brings an entirely new texture and feel to fries. I wouldn't be surprised if these became your go-to side for burgers or steaks.

While they are cooking in the oven, throw together a batch of our Avocado Dipping Sauce (see recipe page 166). Substitute a chipotle pepper in adobo sauce for the Dijon mustard in the dipping sauce recipe to give it a bit more smoky flavor.

1 tablespoon coconut oil

½ teaspoon freshly ground black pepper

¼ teaspoon salt

¼ teaspoon chipotle powder

⅛ teaspoon onion powder

⅛ teaspoon smoked paprika

1 pound jicama, peeled and cut into medium-size fries

NOTE: A mandoline makes quick work of creating your fries.

1. Preheat the oven to 400°F.

2. Heat the coconut oil in an ovenproof glass bowl either in the microwave or in the oven.

3. Combine the pepper, salt, chipotle powder, onion powder and paprika in a small bowl or shaker.

4. Toss the jicama fries in the warm coconut oil to coat, and sprinkle on the seasonings as you go.

5. Place a cooling rack on a sheet pan and spread the fries on it evenly.

6. Bake the jicama fries for 25 to 30 minutes and serve at once.

15 **Active hands-on time**

40 **Total time**

Seasoned Jicama Fries with Avocado Dipping Sauce (page 166)

SESAME ASPARAGUS

Yield: 4-6 servings

Asparagus has long been a staple in my life. My grandmother would make an asparagus casserole every Thanksgiving. We are always looking for new and creative ways to prepare this delicious veggie. Two years ago I got the wild idea to plant some of this stuff in our backyard garden. It is a very resilient plant, which is probably a big reason why it grows all over the world. Unlike most other vegetables, you must wait at least two years before your asparagus plants produce stalks to harvest. We moved houses last year and regrettably left the asparagus behind. I hope the new owner is enjoying it. Now, to get some shoots in the ground at the new casa. — **CHARLES**

1 bunch asparagus spears
(about one pound)

1 teaspoon sesame oil, plus 2 teaspoons
for coating

½ teaspoon dried marjoram

1 medium red bell pepper, seeded,
deribbed and julienned

1 small clove garlic, peeled and minced

½ teaspoon sesame seeds, toasted

NOTE: A little sesame oil goes a long way. While we are believers in guesstimating on many ingredients, be careful, as too much sesame oil can really overpower a dish.

1. Cut the asparagus into 1-inch pieces on the diagonal, discarding the tough, woody ends.

2. Heat 1 teaspoon of the sesame oil over medium heat in a nonstick skillet and add the marjoram.

3. Sauté the asparagus and peppers until the asparagus is dark green and still crisp, being careful not to overcook it.

4. Remove the skillet from the heat, and stir in the garlic and the remaining 2 teaspoons of sesame oil.

5. Garnish the asparagus and peppers with sesame seeds and serve.

5 **Active hands-on time**

15 **Total time**

SWEET AND SAVORY ROASTED CAULIFLOWER

Yield: 6-8 servings

We have our tremendous photographer, Mark, to thank for this recipe. In addition to being an amazing talent who photographs our food, Mark is also a talented musician, a videographer and an all-around cool dude. He plays in a ragtag band of our mutual friends called Yes Ma'am here in Atlanta. One evening we went to listen to them play and met another friend at a restaurant called Holy Taco in East Atlanta Village. Lo and behold, they had a roasted cauliflower dish on their menu that blew our socks off—and this recipe is inspired by that dish. Good music, good friends and a delicious dish to boot. Hard to top an evening like that one.

1 medium head of cauliflower, trimmed into small, bite-size pieces

1 tablespoon olive oil

1 teaspoon ground cumin

½ teaspoon freshly cracked black pepper

¼ cup ghee or coconut oil

¼ cup dates, pitted and finely chopped

1 tablespoon minced fresh rosemary

1 cup pitted black olives, cut in half

NOTES: Any kind of olive will do here, so feel free to use what you have on hand. For ease of cleanup, we suggest coating your sheet pan with aluminum foil first!

1. Preheat the oven to 400°F.

2. Coat the cauliflower pieces with the olive oil, cumin and pepper. Place on a sheet pan in a single layer.

3. Place the sheet pan on the top rack of the oven and roast the cauliflower for 15 minutes, or until lightly browned.

4. Meanwhile, heat the ghee in a small saucepan over medium heat. When the ghee is melted, add the dates and rosemary and cook for 2-3 minutes. Use a spatula to separate the date bits in the ghee as they cook. Remove from the heat and stir in the olives.

5. Remove the cauliflower from the oven and transfer it to a medium-size serving bowl. Add the date-olive mixture and toss gently.

10 **Active hands-on time**

25 **Total time**

TZATZIKI SAUCE

Yield: 1–1½ cups

This sauce is an obvious choice for our Lamb Burgers (see recipe page 90). It is so versatile and can add flavor to most meats and veggies. Make a big batch and serve it with cut vegetables as an appetizer. If you don't have Paleo Mayonnaise sitting around, just increase the amount of coconut milk to ¾ cup. It is a great substitute and will result in almost the same Tzatziki texture.

½ medium cucumber, peeled, seeded and cut into cubes

½ cup Paleo Mayonnaise (see recipe page 204)

¼ cup unsweetened coconut milk

1 tablespoon minced fresh dill (optional)

1 clove garlic, peeled and crushed

1 teaspoon freshly squeezed lemon juice

1 teaspoon onion powder

½ teaspoon freshly ground black pepper

¼ teaspoon salt

1. Combine all the ingredients in a mini food processor and process until no large chunks remain.

2. Use immediately, or store for several days. This is a great make-ahead sauce to serve with burgers or chops.

10 **Active hands-on time**

10 **Total time**

Tzatziki Sauce with Lamb Burgers (page 90)

APPLE-CUCUMBER RELISH

Yield: approximately 2½ cups

This quick, summery, crunchy relish is a perfect accompaniment to chicken or fish, and it's also delicious served on its own as a dip. The only time-consuming part is chopping the ingredients (all the more reason to take a knife skills class!).

1 Granny Smith apple, peeled, cored and diced

1 cup peeled, diced English cucumber

½ cup diced jicama

2 tablespoons unsweetened apple cider or apple juice

2 tablespoons fresh lime juice

2 tablespoons very finely minced red onion

½ tablespoon minced fresh flat-leaf (Italian) parsley

1. Combine all the ingredients in a medium bowl and mix well.

2. Serve immediately, or cover and refrigerate until ready to serve.

 VARIATIONS: We once grew some lemon cucumbers in our garden, which would be fantastic in this dish! Adding some red peppers for color would be super tasty, as well.

10 **Active hands-on time**

10 **Total time**

Apple-Cucumber Relish with
Macadamia Nut-Crusted Mahimahi (page 92)

APPLE AND PEAR SAUCE

Yield: approximately 4 cups

During my pregnancy, I couldn't get enough of tart and sour foods, and this recipe was the cure for those cravings. I'm sure there is some wives' tale out there indicating that such cravings meant I was having a boy. This recipe is super easy and superfast—the only part that's at all time-consuming is letting the Apple and Pear Sauce chill in the freezer/refrigerator. Obviously, placing it in the freezer will expedite the chilling process, so if you're in a hurry, opt for that chilling method, and place the sauce in a container with a large surface area to further speed things along. This sauce is like applesauce, only with the added sweetness of pears. It "pears" (yes, you can groan at that one!) well with dishes like the Stuffed Pork Chops (see recipe page 160) and the Almond-Crusted Pork Tenderloin (see recipe page 80). This dish is sure to be a favorite of the kids, too! — *JULIE*

4 Granny Smith apples, peeled, cored and diced

4 ripe pears, peeled, cored and diced

¼ cup water

Juice of 1 lemon

2 teaspoons ground cinnamon

NOTE: You can use any kind of apples you'd like for this recipe, but I personally love the tartness of Granny Smith apples.

1. Place all the ingredients in a medium-size saucepan over medium-high heat, and bring to a boil.

2. Reduce the heat and simmer, covered, until the apples and pears are soft.

3. Using an immersion blender, a regular blender or a food processor, puree the mixture until no lumps remain.

4. Place in the refrigerator or the freezer to cool, but do not let the Apple and Pear Sauce freeze. Serve chilled.

5 **Active hands-on time**

30 **Total time**

BACON AND OKRA PILAU

Yield: 8-10 servings

Pilau (pronounced PEE-low, PER-low, pih-LOW or pur-LOO, depending upon who you talk to in the Georgia and Carolina low country) is essentially a rice pilaf dish. Very often it's served with chicken or seafood, making it a great one-dish meal, but it also makes a wonderful side dish, as we've done here. Don't let the okra scare you: this Southern veggie staple is a key component to this dish (in our opinion) and the slimy factor just about disappears in this preparation.

4 bacon strips, cut into ½-inch pieces

1 onion, peeled and diced

1 medium green bell pepper, seeded, deribbed and diced

2 cups okra, cut crosswise into ½-inch rounds

3 cups Cauliflower Rice (see How to Make Cauliflower Rice page 45)

½ teaspoon paprika

¼ teaspoon cayenne pepper

Salt and freshly ground black pepper, to taste

1½ cups chicken stock

1. Preheat a Dutch oven or a large skillet (with a lid) over medium heat, add the bacon and fry until crispy. Using a slotted spoon, remove the bacon from the Dutch oven to a plate lined with paper towels. Reserve the bacon grease in the Dutch oven.

2. Add the onions and peppers to the Dutch oven in which the bacon was fried and sauté for 4 to 6 minutes, or until the onions soften. Mix in the okra, increase the heat to medium-high and then stir in the Cauliflower Rice, paprika, cayenne pepper, salt and pepper.

3. Pour in the chicken stock, cover, and bring to a boil. Reduce the heat to low, cover and let simmer until most of the chicken stock has cooked off, about 10 minutes.

4. Mix in the reserved bacon and serve hot.

10-15 **Active hands-on time**

25 **Total time**

BAGNA CÀUDA

Yield: approximately ¾ cup

It is not a secret that we are *superfans* of sauces. They can take the ordinary to the extraordinary. The name *bagna càuda* literally means "hot bath," and while there are different stories about its origins and background—some say it was a morning snack for vineyard workers on cold days, while others say it was a celebratory snack after the harvest in the vineyards—the one certainty about this sauce is that it's to be shared, ideally among a gathering of friends, with a variety of farm-fresh vegetables for dipping. What's not to love about *that!?*

You are probably thinking that anchovies might taste a little…gross…in this recipe. I hear what you are saying, but I implore you to try this just once. Take some roasted broccoli or cauliflower and toss it with this sauce, or dip raw veggies in this hot bath.

½ cup extra-virgin olive oil

¼ cup ghee

6 large cloves garlic, peeled and minced

One 2-ounce tin anchovies

¼ teaspoon salt

1. Combine all the ingredients in a small saucepan and cook over low heat, for about 10 minutes, allowing the flavors to meld.

2. Mash up the anchovies with a fork until they have disintegrated in the oil/ghee mixture.

3. Serve hot.

NOTES: A garlic press makes very quick work of mincing the garlic. A squeeze or two of lemon juice would brighten up this sauce that much more.

5 **Active hands-on time**

15 **Total time**

BASIL PESTO

Yield: approximately ⅔ cup

When our garden is overflowing with basil in the summertime, you'll always find a jar or two of pesto in our refrigerator. Pesto spaghetti squash, pesto zucchini noodles, pesto chicken, pesto shrimp, pesto salmon . . . Needless to say, we think pesto goes with just about anything!

2½ cups fresh basil leaves (packed)

½ cup olive oil

¼ cup pine nuts or walnuts, toasted

2 cloves garlic, peeled

Salt and freshly ground black pepper, to taste

1. Combine all the ingredients in a food processor and blend until smooth.

NOTES: If you'd like to keep your pesto extra bright green (and you have a few extra minutes), blanch the basil leaves in a pot of boiling water for about 60 seconds, and then transfer the leaves to an ice-water bath to stop the cooking. See page 204 for a super-simple basil aioli recipe. Or even easier, just stir about a ½ cup of Paleo Mayonnaise (see recipe page 204) into the Basil Pesto to make a quick basil mayonnaise. (The difference being that the aioli has no nuts in it).

5 **Active hands-on time**

5 **Total time**

CHIPOTLE MASHED SWEET POTATOES

Yield: 8-10 servings

Smoky and sweet, that's what this combination of chipotles and sweet potatoes is. This side dish is a great pairing with simple grilled steaks or pork chops or chicken, or really with just about anything, in our opinion!

3 pounds sweet potatoes, peeled and cut into 1-inch cubes

½ cup unsweetened coconut milk

¼ cup chicken stock

3 teaspoons minced canned chipotle peppers in adobo sauce

3 tablespoons ghee (optional)

NOTES: To make this dish even quicker, place the sweet potatoes in a microwave-safe glass bowl, and microwave on high for 8 to 10 minutes, or until sweet potatoes are fork-tender. Though it involves an extra piece of equipment, you can also steam your sweet potatoes (versus boiling them) by using a steamer basket inside a pot.

 VARIATION: Some sprinkles of cinnamon would be a nice addition to these smoky sweet potatoes.

1. Place the sweet potatoes in a large pot, cover with water and bring to a boil over medium-high heat. Reduce the heat and cook for 15 to 20 minutes, or until the sweet potatoes are fork-tender. Pour the sweet potatoes into a colander to drain.

2. Place the sweet potatoes in a large bowl and add the coconut milk, chicken stock, chipotle peppers and ghee, if desired. With a potato masher, hand mixer or immersion blender, mash the sweet potatoes. You could also process in a food processor. If you prefer your mashed sweet potatoes a bit thinner, simply add more coconut milk or chicken stock.

5 **Active hands-on time**

20-25 **Total time**

CURRY NOODLES

Yield: 4–6 servings

Noodles in all forms seem to scream comfort. It's no surprise that this is one food most people say they miss the most when they adopt a Paleo lifestyle. Lucky for us, noodles don't have to contain starch or gluten. Enter the veggie noodles! The fastest and easiest way we've found to create "noodles" with our vegetables is to invest less than twenty dollars in a julienne peeler. This simple tool makes easy work of creating your "noodles," and if you have little helpers in the kitchen, it's a great way to get them involved as sous-chefs.

2 teaspoons oil or cooking fat of choice

1 tablespoon red or panang curry paste

2 cups unsweetened coconut milk

2 to 3 large zucchini squash, ends cut off and julienned into "noodles" (discard the center part, which is mostly seeds)

2 to 3 yellow summer squash, julienned into "noodles" (discard the center part, which is mostly seeds)

1 large red bell pepper, seeded, deribbed and cut into long strips

2 teaspoons coconut aminos

1. Heat the oil and curry paste over medium heat in a large skillet, using the back of a spatula or spoon to smear the curry paste into the oil. When the paste has become very fragrant, add the coconut milk and stir to combine well.

2. Add the zucchini, yellow squash, peppers and coconut aminos and cook for 5 to 10 minutes, or until the squash has softened slightly.

NOTES: Of course you can scale up or down the amount of curry paste, depending on your taste. If you like your curry dishes extra hot, why not add some chopped up Thai chilies to the mix? To make this an entrée, go ahead and add about 2 pounds of your favorite cooked protein.

5 **Active hands-on time**

15 **Total time**

GARLICKY BUTTERED CABBAGE NOODLES

Yield: 4-6 servings

This is one of those amazingly simple dishes that we almost feel guilty about including. And yet sometimes simpler is better. These noodles go with just about anything in our house, and we usually try to keep a container or two in the fridge as a quick go-to side dish.

1 tablespoon coconut oil

5 to 6 cloves garlic, peeled, minced (divided in half)

½ head green cabbage, sliced thin

3 tablespoons ghee

Salt and freshly ground black pepper, to taste

NOTE: If you feel that your cabbage needs more flavor, add some smoked paprika.

 VARIATIONS: Red cabbage would also be great here, or a mix of the two for a very colorful side.

1. Heat the coconut oil over medium heat in a large frying pan or skillet that is already hot. Once the oil is hot, add half the garlic and sauté for about 30 seconds, being careful not to burn it. Add the cabbage and sauté until softened, about 5 minutes.

2. Add the remaining garlic and the ghee, mix well, and cook for 2 or 3 minutes to allow the flavors to combine. Season with salt and pepper, to taste.

5 **Active hands-on time**

15 **Total time**

GINGER-GLAZED CARROTS

Yield: 4-6 servings

Carrots don't typically do much for us on their own. Usually we prefer dipping them into something. This dish changed our opinion of these taproots. Furthermore, cooking carrots increases their levels of beta-carotene, and that's always a good thing.

2 tablespoons coconut oil or ghee

1 pound carrots, peeled and cut diagonally into ¼-inch slices

½ cup chicken or vegetable stock

1 teaspoon minced fresh ginger

1 teaspoon ground ginger

½ teaspoon chili powder

½ teaspoon salt

1 tablespoon chopped fresh flat-leaf (Italian) parsley

NOTE: If your local farmers' markets carry carrots in assorted colors, by all means go for those, as that would make this a super-colorful dish!

1. Heat the oil over medium heat in a large skillet or a medium-size pot that is already hot. When the oil is hot, stir in the carrots, stock and fresh ginger. Cover and simmer for about 5 to 10 minutes, or until the stock has almost fully evaporated.

2. Stir in the ground ginger, chili powder and salt and cook until the carrots are soft, but not totally mushy. Sprinkle with parsley and serve immediately.

5 **Active hands-on time**

20 **Total time**

HOLLANDAISE SAUCE

Yield: approximately ½ cup

Perhaps most commonly thought of as an accompaniment to eggs Benedict, hollandaise sauce goes great on top of salmon or vegetables, such as Brussels sprouts, artichokes, broccoli, green beans and more. I have many memories of my mom making hollandaise to serve over asparagus to dress it up a bit, and I wish I had had the palate for hollandaise then like I do now! — *JULIE*

2 large egg yolks

2 teaspoons cold water

1 tablespoon freshly squeezed lemon juice, divided

½ cup ghee, melted (but not hot)

Salt, to taste

Cayenne pepper, paprika or Tabasco sauce, to taste

NOTE: Sometimes the Hollandaise Sauce can get overheated, causing it to break down. If this happens, you can try adding a little bit of cold water, a bit at a time, whisking it into your sauce.

1. In a medium saucepan, heat about 2 inches of water to a gentle simmer.

2. Meanwhile, in a heatproof glass or aluminum bowl, whisk together the egg yolks, the 2 teaspoons cold water and a few drops of lemon juice. Whisk until foamy and light.

3. Making sure the bottom of the bowl does not come in contact with the water, place the bowl with the egg yolks over the simmering water (essentially creating a water bath) and continuously whisk the yolks until they have thickened, about 1 to 2 minutes.

4. Remove the bowl from the heat and ever so slowly (we're serious, *super* slowly) begin adding in drops of ghee, whisking the whole time. Continue adding the ghee (you can increase the speed at which you add the drops as the mixture starts to thicken) until all of it has been mixed in.

5. Mix in the remaining lemon juice, salt, and cayenne pepper, paprika or Tabasco sauce, if desired.

15 **Active hands-on time**

15 **Total time**

VARIATION: You can convert your hollandaise into a "quick and easy" béarnaise sauce by adding roughly 1 tablespoon minced fresh tarragon and 1 tablespoon finely diced shallots. Note that true béarnaise sauce typically involves a slightly different process (simmering the shallots and tarragon in vinegar in place of the lemon juice in the hollandaise). You could go that route, too, but this way may be easier!

PALEO MAYONNAISE AND TWO AIOLIS

**Yield: approximately 1 cup of the master mayonnaise
(double the recipe if you wish to have mayo on hand or to create the aiolis)**

While we included a recipe for mayo in *Paleo Comfort Foods,* it's such a frequently used condiment that we felt it necessary to include it again, though this time there are some variations, along with the tasty aiolis, which you can make from one mayo recipe!

FOR THE PALEO MAYONNAISE:

2 large egg yolks

½ teaspoon salt

¼ teaspoon Dijon mustard

2 teaspoons freshly squeezed lemon juice

1½ teaspoons white vinegar

1 cup mild-tasting oil (light extra-virgin olive oil, macadamia nut oil, avocado oil or a combination of oils)

1. In a food processor, combine the egg yolks, salt and Dijon mustard.

2. Add the lemon juice and vinegar and blend until bright yellow.

3. Slowly (drop by drop) with the processor running, add the oil. Once the mayo seems to have thickened some, you can be a little more liberal with the oil, still adding it only in a gentle stream. In less than 5 minutes you should have a thick, creamy mayo.

FOR THE BASIL AIOLI:

¾ cup basil leaves (loosely packed)

1 tablespoon olive oil

1 clove garlic, peeled and crushed

½ cup Paleo Mayonnaise

Salt and freshly ground black pepper, to taste

1. Pulse the basil, olive oil and garlic in a food processor until the basil leaves are finely minced.

2. Add the mayonnaise and blend until well combined. Season with salt and pepper, to taste.

FOR THE LEMON-CAPER AIOLI:

1 tablespoon capers, drained

1 clove garlic, peeled and crushed

1 tablespoon olive oil

2 teaspoons freshly squeezed lemon juice

½ cup Paleo Mayonnaise

1. Pulse the capers, garlic, olive oil and lemon juice in a food processor until the capers and garlic are finely minced.

2. Add the mayonnaise and blend until well combined.

NOTE: These should keep refrigerated for a few days.

5 **Active hands-on time**

10 **Total time**

From top to bottom: Basil Aioli,
Paleo Mayonnaise, Lemon-Caper Aioli

VARIATIONS: Of course, there are so many
other aioli variations you could make.
Plain garlic aioli, chipotle aioli, truffle aioli,
parsley aioli, even a bacon aioli. Experiment
to make your own signature sauce!

PEACH SALSA

Yield: 1½–2 cups

Georgia is the Peach State, so it seemed completely fitting that we include at least one peach dish in our book! And knowing our penchant for sauces—especially sauces with a kick—a peach salsa seemed like the perfect one to include. This salsa makes a great accompaniment to salmon, pork or chicken and works deliciously well served on top of some fresh fish tacos.

Not all jalapeños are created equal! Get one superhot jalapeño, and it will make this some really fiery salsa. Yet other jalapeños are so mild, you'd think you were eating bell peppers. According to some old kitchen tales for choosing hotter peppers, you should look for ones with small white lines (called corking) that emanate near the stem, or you should choose peppers grown during particularly dry summers. Some say red jalapeños are hotter; others say they are milder. I usually just cut off a teeny bit of the pepper and taste it before using it in a dish. If I can eat it, it usually means it's about as mild as a sweet pepper. If it sets my mouth on fire, then Charles usually says it's mild! — *JULIE*

3 to 4 medium peaches, pitted and diced

2 plum tomatoes, seeded and diced

½ cup diced sweet onion (such as Vidalia, Bermuda or Sweet Maui)

1 fresh jalapeño pepper, seeded and finely diced

Juice of 1 lime

2 tablespoons minced fresh cilantro

2 tablespoons minced fresh mint

1. Combine all the ingredients in medium-size bowl.

2. Cover and keep refrigerated until ready to serve.

10 **Active hands-on time**

10 **Total time**

NOTE: Cut-up peaches mixed with lime juice start to lose their color and fresh look pretty quickly, though the taste is still fine. We suggest serving this salsa on the same day you make it or holding off on adding the lime juice until you are going to serve this.

ROASTED MASHED PARSNIPS

Yield: 4-6 servings

Why we didn't grow up eating parsnips is beyond us. These mashed parsnips are almost candy-like, and the caramelization adds a delicious flavor. Next time you're thinking about making mashed cauliflower, add in some roasted parsnips for a sweet little twist.

2 pounds parsnips, peeled and cut into small cubes

2 tablespoons olive oil

1 to 1½ cups chicken stock

2 tablespoons ghee

Salt and freshly ground black pepper, to taste

NOTE: If you really want to emphasize the sweetness of the parsnips, add some cinnamon or nutmeg to the puree.

1. Preheat the oven to 400°F.

2. Place the parsnips on a sheet pan and drizzle with the olive oil, using your hands to evenly coat them. Roast the parsnips in the oven for 20 to 25 minutes, or until they are somewhat caramelized around the edges, turning them over midway through cooking.

3. Transfer the parsnips to a food processor, along with half of the chicken stock and the ghee. Puree and check the consistency. If you prefer a thinner puree, add more chicken stock to achieve your desired consistency. Season with salt and pepper, to taste.

5 **Active hands-on time**

30 **Total time**

ROOT VEGGIE CAKES

Yield: 16-20 cakes

These are like root vegetable latkes, with some sweetness from the parsnips and carrots, a little kick from the horseradish and some earthiness from the beets. We love topping these with a dollop of prepared horseradish mixed with some home-made mayo for an extra kick!

2 large eggs, beaten

½ cup almond, coconut or sweet potato flour

3 medium scallions, sliced thinly on the bias

2 tablespoons prepared horseradish

½ teaspoon salt

½ teaspoon freshly ground black pepper

2 cups shredded carrots

2 cups shredded parsnips

1 cup shredded beets

Oil or cooking fat of choice, for sautéing

NOTE: Be sure to read the label on your horseradish, as not all brands are created equal and many contain soybean oil.

EQUIPMENT NOTE: This is one of those recipes where a shred blade on a food processor makes your life infinitely easier. While, sure, you could hand shred the vegetables, it literally takes less than 5 minutes to shred them with your food processor!

1. Preheat the oven to 300°F.

2. Mix together the eggs, flour, scallions, horseradish, salt and pepper in a large mixing bowl. Stir in the vegetables and combine well.

3. Heat 1 tablespoon oil in a large skillet over medium-high heat.

4. Fill a measuring cup (¼ cup or ⅓ cup is suggested) to the top with the root vegetable mixture and invert on the skillet, forming a flat patty (use a spatula to press down and flatten). Repeat until there are 4 or 5 patties in the skillet. Brown for 3 to 4 minutes per side, or until slightly crispy. Remove the patties to a sheet pan and place them in the oven to keep warm. Repeat the procedure, adding more oil with each batch, until all the root vegetable mixture is used.

5. Serve hot from the oven.

15 **Active hands-on time**

30 **Total time**

VARIATIONS: Use turnips, sweet potatoes, or any other roots or tubers you'd like to try in this dish! Bacon would, of course, taste wonderful mixed into these, as well.

SAUSAGE AND APPLE DRESSING

Yield: 6–8 servings

Here in America, one dish you'll pretty much see only in November is stuffing, or dressing (pretty sure there have been many lively family discussions about whether it should be called stuffing or dressing). As there are food safety concerns about undercooking the dressing if it is cooked inside the turkey—or worse, cooking the stuffing enough but overcooking the turkey—we find it safest to serve this dish on the side as a dressing. While we've also made this dressing using some Paleo bread cubes made from a Paleo loaf of bread, we found that you really won't miss bread in this dressing at all.

1 pound ground pork

2 teaspoons minced fresh sage leaves

1 teaspoon minced fresh thyme

¼ teaspoon finely minced fresh rosemary

¼ teaspoon cayenne pepper

¼ teaspoon crushed red pepper flakes

2 tablespoons oil or cooking fat of choice

3 cups diced celery

2 cups diced onion

1 pound button or cremini mushrooms, cleaned and diced

3 Granny Smith apples, cored and diced

2 tablespoons poultry seasoning

Salt and freshly ground black pepper, to taste

2 large eggs

¼ cup turkey stock or drippings from turkey

1. Preheat the oven to 350°F.

2. In a large skillet, combine the pork, sage, thyme, rosemary, cayenne pepper and red pepper flakes. Brown the pork over medium heat, mixing well and breaking up the pork into small bits as it cooks. When the pork is cooked through, transfer it to an 11 x 13-inch baking dish and set aside.

3. In the skillet in which the pork was cooked, heat the oil over medium heat. Add the celery, onions, mushrooms and apples and cook until the onions are translucent and the celery and mushrooms have softened somewhat. Mix in the poultry seasoning, salt and pepper.

4. In a small bowl, whisk together the eggs and turkey stock. Set aside.

5. Stir the sautéed vegetables into the reserved pork in the baking dish and pour the egg/stock mixture over the top.

6. Bake, uncovered, for 15 to 20 minutes, or until the dressing is somewhat browned on top.

10 **Active hands-on time**

30 **Total time**

NOTE: In step 2, you're basically making your own sausage. If you have an already prepared sausage that you like that isn't full of additives, feel free to use that instead, thereby avoiding the need for the ground pork, sage, thyme, rosemary, cayenne pepper and red pepper flakes listed in the recipe.

NOTE: Don't have poultry seasoning on hand? Most poultry seasonings are a blend of predominantly sage, thyme and marjoram, with lesser amounts of rosemary, celery seed and sometimes savory. If you have any of these dried herbs on hand, simply blend them up in a spice grinder to create your own poultry seasoning.

SAUTÉED BRUSSELS SPROUTS

Yield: 4–6 servings

True story: Brussels sprouts were served at our baby shower (hosted by dear friends at our favorite dining destination in Atlanta, Local Three). Fortunately, executive chef and Paleo convert Chris Hall knew our love for these mini cabbage heads and made sure they were on the menu for the festivities. (Also on the menu was Charles's favorite, Local Three's amazing steak tartare.) We don't own a deep-fat fryer filled with duck fat (part of what makes this dish stand out at Local Three), but here we do our best to replicate the dish at home with a few modifications.

6 bacon strips

¼ cup duck fat (if you have it), or use coconut oil, bacon grease or lard

2 pounds Brussels sprouts, trimmed and halved

1 tablespoon sherry vinegar

2 teaspoons minced fresh rosemary

Salt and freshly ground black pepper, to taste

EQUIPMENT NOTE: For an even faster cooking time, shred the raw Brussels sprouts with the slicing blade of your food processor.

1. In a large skillet or frying pan, cook the bacon over medium heat until it is crispy. Remove the bacon to a large plate, allow it to cool and cut it into small pieces. Set aside. Reserve the bacon drippings in the skillet.

2. To the skillet in which the bacon was cooked, add the duck fat and increase the heat to medium-high. Carefully add the Brussels sprouts (take caution, as the fat may splatter) and cook, stirring occasionally, until they begin to crisp up, about 5 to 7 minutes. Transfer the Brussels sprouts to a large bowl.

3. Toss the hot Brussels sprouts with the reserved bacon, sherry vinegar, rosemary, salt and pepper. Serve hot!

10 **Active hands-on time**

20 **Total time**

SAUTÉED KALE WITH A KICK

Yield: 6-8 servings

Truth be told, cooked kale was not my favorite vegetable during my pregnancy, as its earthy flavor combined with my changing taste buds had me likening its flavor to dirt. Yet during my pregnancy, I kept reading about what a superfood kale is, and how it is such a great source of folate. In addition to trying to "hide" kale in soups, stews and even my morning eggs, I wanted to find ways to prepare the leafy green so that it tasted good on its own. That's how this recipe came about. Something about adding a kick to the greens made them taste that much better! — *JULIE*

2 teaspoons oil or cooking fat of choice

1 medium yellow onion, peeled and sliced

1 to 2 red or green jalapeño peppers, seeded (if preferred) and sliced into ⅛-inch thick rings

2 cloves garlic, peeled and minced

1 pound kale, stems removed and chopped

1 cup chicken stock

½ teaspoon salt

¼ teaspoon freshly ground black pepper

NOTE: If "with a kick" doesn't work for you, simply leave out the jalapeños.

1. Heat the oil in a large Dutch oven or soup pot over medium-high heat. Add the onions and jalapeños, and sauté until the onions are slightly translucent, about 4 minutes. Add the garlic and sauté until just fragrant.

2. Add the kale, chicken stock, salt and pepper and reduce the heat to medium-low. Cover and cook for 10 to 15 minutes, or until the kale is tender.

5 **Active hands-on time**

25 **Total time**

VARIATIONS: Some tomatoes or mushrooms would be welcome additions to this dish. You can use any kind of kale you'd like, or if collard greens are more accessible to you, use those.

SPICY PLUM SAUCE

Yield: 1 cup

We had some venison tenderloin just waiting to be cooked, and this sauce accompaniment seemed a perfect pairing. Truth be told, I think this sauce would go great with just about any cut of meat! It keeps well in the refrigerator for several days, so you can opt for a variety of meats to pair with it. — *JULIE*

2 New Mexico chilies or other chilies, stems removed, seeded and roughly chopped

2 plums, pitted and cut into quarters

½ cup chopped onion

½ cup water

2 tablespoons apple cider vinegar

Juice of 1 lime

1 clove garlic, peeled and coarsely chopped

NOTE: It is not critical to strain the sauce, but I find that the bits of pepper and plum skins can be a little bitter.

1. Heat a small saucepan over medium heat. Once it is hot, add the chilies and toast for about 2 minutes, or until just aromatic, being careful not to burn them.

2. Add the plums, onions, water, vinegar, lime juice and garlic and bring to a simmer.

3. Reduce the heat to medium-low and cook until the mixture thickens, about 10 to 15 minutes.

4. Pour the mixture into a blender, and process until no large chunks remain. Strain the mixture through a chinois or fine mesh strainer. Serve the sauce warm.

5 **Active hands-on time**

20 **Total time**

Spicy Plum Sauce with Almond-Crusted Pork Tenderloin (page 80)

SUMMER SQUASH SAUTÉ

Yield: 6–8 servings

I used to have a bit of disdain for the squash in our garden, mostly because the plants took up so much room! However, the perk of growing your own vegetables is that you then have the bounty to cook up in dishes like this. With the exception of the onions and garlic, this is one of those dishes entirely sourced from our garden, and that makes me wish for summertime year-round! — *JULIE*

2 tablespoons oil or cooking fat of choice

1 medium yellow onion, peeled and sliced

2 pounds yellow and/or zucchini squash, halved lengthwise and sliced into ¼-inch half-moons

2 large tomatoes (heirloom or vine-ripened), cut into wedges

3 cloves garlic, peeled and minced

2 tablespoons minced fresh basil

Salt and freshly ground black pepper, to taste

1. Heat the oil over medium heat in a large skillet that is already hot. Once the oil is hot, add the onions and sauté until translucent, about 4 to 6 minutes.

2. Add the squash, tomatoes, garlic, basil, salt and pepper, and cook until the squash is somewhat tender and the tomatoes have started to break down, about 4 to 5 minutes.

 VARIATIONS: Mushrooms would go well with this combination, as would just about any other vegetables you can think of. Eat dairy? Top this dish off with some fresh Parmesan cheese to make it a little more indulgent.

5 **Active hands-on time**

20 **Total time**

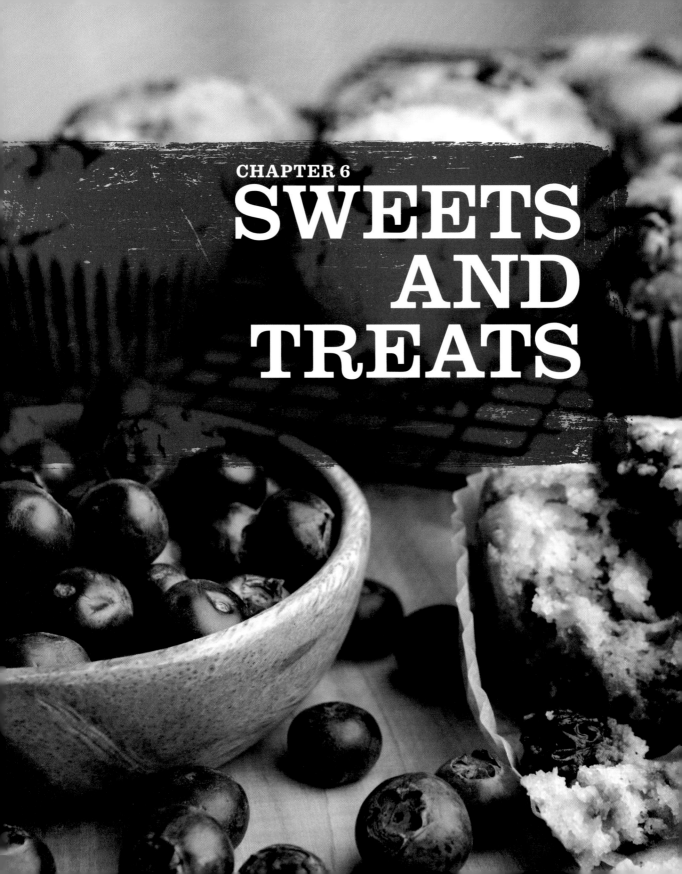

CHAPTER 6

SWEETS AND TREATS

Banana Muffins 224

Berry Scones 226

Blueberry Muffins 228

Homemade "LÄRABAR" Balls, Three Ways 230

Lemony Cookies 234

Molasses Ginger Cookies 236

Not Nutella 238

Plantains with Coconut 240

BANANA MUFFINS

Yield: 12 muffins

Don't throw those brown bananas away. . . Make something delicious out of them. Seriously, you want bananas that are overripe for this recipe—the peel should be nearly all brown. They will be practically mushy to the touch and will bring so much flavor to these light and fluffy treats, you won't know what hit you. Banana muffins are great to pack in a school lunch for the kids or to have as an easy "go-to" snack. If you are enjoying these a day or two after making them, cut them in half and microwave them with a touch of butter or coconut butter for a sweet and decadent snack.

Oil, for greasing the muffin tin

1½ cups almond meal

½ cup chopped pecans

1 teaspoon ground cinnamon

1½ teaspoons baking soda

¼ teaspoon ground nutmeg

2 large eggs

3 ripe bananas, mashed

¼ cup applesauce (no sugar added)

1 teaspoon vanilla extract

NOTES: You can also make a loaf of banana bread by pouring the batter into a greased 9 x 5 x 3-inch loaf pan. Just bake about 10 to 20 minutes longer, or until a toothpick inserted into the center comes out clean.

1. Preheat the oven to 350°F. Grease the wells of a 12-cup muffin tin with oil.

2. Mix the almond meal, pecans, cinnamon, baking soda and nutmeg in medium-size mixing bowl.

3. In a separate medium-size bowl, whisk the eggs. Stir in the bananas, applesauce and vanilla and mix until just combined.

4. Fold the dry ingredients into the wet ingredients, being careful not to overmix, and then spoon the batter into the wells of the greased muffin tin.

5. Bake for 15 to 20 minutes, or until a toothpick inserted in the middle of each muffin comes out clean.

10 **Active hands-on time**

30 **Total time**

VARIATION: Walnuts are also a nice option.

BERRY SCONES

Yield: 10–12 scones

In a former life (okay, not that long ago), I was a sucker for the bakery display case at _____ (insert name of your favorite coffee shop). Muffins, cakes and scones... ah, yes, scones. Raisin scones, cinnamon scones and my personal favorite: any of the berry scones. Sad to say, these treats weren't "treating" my health (or my bank account) all that well. It had been years since I'd had a scone, when we came up with this gluten-free variation for the book. These cook quickly and tend to disappear even faster... so be sure to eat these in moderation! — *JULIE*

Parchment paper, for lining the sheet pan

2½ cups blanched almond flour (we prefer the Honeyville brand)

1 tablespoon plus 1 teaspoon coconut sugar

2 teaspoons baking soda

1 teaspoon lemon zest

Pinch of salt

¼ cup ghee or coconut oil, at room temperature

2 large eggs

2 teaspoons vanilla extract

1 cup fresh raspberries

1. Preheat the oven to 350°F. Line a sheet pan with parchment paper.

2. In a medium-size mixing bowl, whisk together the almond flour, coconut sugar, baking powder, lemon zest and salt. Add the ghee and, using a fork or your fingers, combine until the mixture resembles coarse meal.

3. Add the eggs and vanilla and mix. Gently fold in the berries.

4. Form the dough into 12 scones of equal size (the triangle shape is typical, but you can shape these however you'd like) and place them on the prepared sheet pan.

5. Bake the scones for approximately 15 minutes, or until golden brown around the edges.

NOTE: If you don't have access to coconut sugar, use 1 tablespoon raw honey instead. However, instead of adding the honey in step 2, when the coconut sugar is added, add the honey in step 3, along with the eggs and vanilla.

5 **Active hands-on time**

25 **Total time**

VARIATIONS: Don't feel like raspberries? You can use other fresh berries (strawberries, blueberries, blackberries), or even give these a shot with some dried fruit (raisins, cranberries, etc.).

BLUEBERRY MUFFINS

Yield: 12 muffins

Back in the day, I was quite the baker. I loved making several dozen muffins using my family's favorite blueberry muffin recipe to share with friends in high school. Enter Paleo, and my desire to bake, my experimentation with baking, and my arsenal of baking supplies dwindled significantly. I just didn't have the desire to bake a lot of treats, and I knew I was healthier for it (as were my friends). However, blueberry muffins still call my name every once in a while, and this recipe is the answer to that. — *JULIE*

12 paper muffin tin liners

3 cups almond flour

1 teaspoon ground cinnamon

¾ teaspoon baking soda

¼ teaspoon salt

3 large eggs

⅓ cup coconut oil, melted slightly

¼ cup unsweetened coconut milk

2 tablespoons honey or maple syrup (optional)

1½ cups fresh blueberries

1. Preheat the oven to 375°F, and line the wells of a 12-cup muffin tin with paper liners.

2. In a large mixing bowl, combine the almond flour, cinnamon, baking soda and salt and mix well.

3. Add the eggs, coconut oil, coconut milk and honey and mix thoroughly. Gently fold in the blueberries.

4. Carefully spoon the batter into the prepared muffin tin, so that each well is about ¾ full.

5. Bake for 20 to 25 minutes, or until a toothpick inserted into the middle of each muffin comes out clean.

NOTES: While frozen blueberries oftentimes have a lot more flavor than fresh (as they are typically picked before they are overripe), we still prefer to use fresh blueberries. A tip if you are using frozen: take them out of the freezer at the very last second and quickly toss them with coconut or almond flour before gently mixing them into your batter.

5–10 **Active hands-on time**

30 **Total time**

HOMEMADE "LÄRABAR" BALLS, THREE WAYS

LÄRABARs have been my emergency go-to staple for many cross-country flights, weeks at summer camp, or times when I knew it might be challenging to find any snacks to tide me over until the next meal. It seemed like a no-brainer to go ahead and try our hand at making some mini versions of the same, as these make for the perfect snack or treat when you're craving something sweet. Here are three of our favorite varieties to make. — *JULIE*

DATE BALLS

Yield: 10–12 balls

¾ cup pitted dates

⅓ cup walnuts

⅓ cup unsalted cashews

¼ cup unsweetened shredded coconut

1. Combine all the ingredients in the food processor and process until well blended, about 30 to 60 seconds. Check to make sure the mixture will hold together when pressed between your fingertips. If it's too dry, add 1 to 2 teaspoons water and process a bit longer.

2. Using clean hands, take a small amount of the date mixture and roll it into a Ping-Pong ball–size ball (you can actually make these as big or small as you'd like!). Repeat until all the date mixture has been rolled into balls.

3. Store the Date Balls in an airtight container for up to several days (or until you devour them all!).

5 Active hands-on time

5 Total time

NUTLESS BALLS

Yield: 16–20 balls

¾ cup pitted dates

½ cup sunflower seeds

½ cup unsweetened shredded coconut

1 to 2 teaspoons water

NOTES: As a general rule, too many nuts (or too much of anything, for that matter) can negatively impact your health. To minimize the amount of phytic acid in the nuts used in these date balls, you can soak the nuts in water for 18 hours, dehydrate them in a food dehydrator or a low-temperature oven, and then roast them.

That being said, these are indeed some sweet treats, and they are not meant to be consumed all the time or in copious amounts, so if you are eating them in moderation and have minimized your other sources of phytic acid (non-soaked nuts and seeds), you should be okay!

1. Combine the dates, sunflower seeds, coconut and 1 teaspoon of the water in a food processor. Process for 30 to 60 seconds, or until the mixture is well combined. If the mixture won't hold together when you pinch a small amount between your fingertips, add more water and process a bit longer.

2. Using clean hands, take a small amount of the date mixture and roll it into a Ping-Pong ball–size ball. Repeat until all the date mixture has been rolled into balls.

3. Store the Nutless Balls in an airtight container until ready to serve or snack upon.

5 **Active hands-on time**

5 **Total time**

ISLAND BALLS

Yield: 16–20 balls

1 cup macadamia nuts

¾ cup pitted dates

½ cup unsweetened shredded coconut

¼ cup unsweetened shredded
    coconut, toasted

1. Combine the macadamia nuts, dates and the ½ cup coconut in a food processor and process until well blended, about 30 to 60 seconds.

2. Check to make sure the mixture will hold together when pressed between your fingertips. If it's too dry, add more dates and process in the food processor.

3. Using clean hands, take a small amount of the date mixture and roll it into a Ping-Pong ball–size ball (or bigger or smaller, if you'd like). Repeat until all the date mixture has been rolled into balls.

4. Roll the balls in the ¼ cup toasted coconut to coat.

5. Store the Island Balls in an airtight container until ready to serve or snack upon.

5 **Active hands-on time**

5 **Total time**

Island Balls, Date Balls and Nutless Balls

LEMONY COOKIES

Yield: 12–16 cookies

There's something about lemon that is very soothing. Maybe it's because anytime you're sick, someone invariably suggests lemon water, lemon tea or something else that's lemony. These cookies are a perfect way to get a wee bit of a dessert fix (without much sugar), along with a lemon fix—and a tasty one at that!

Parchment paper, for lining the sheet pan

1 large egg

2 tablespoons honey or maple syrup (or more if you prefer sweeter cookies)

2 tablespoons coconut oil or ghee, melted

2 teaspoons freshly squeezed lemon juice

½ teaspoon vanilla extract

2 cups almond flour

1 tablespoon lemon zest

¼ teaspoon baking soda

 VARIATIONS: Feel free to use some orange in addition to or in place of the lemon. Or some dried fruit (apricots, raisins) added would taste great, too!

1. Preheat the oven to 350°F. Line a sheet pan with parchment paper.

2. In a small mixing bowl, mix together the egg, honey or maple syrup, coconut oil or ghee, lemon juice, and vanilla extract. In a medium-size mixing bowl, mix together the almond flour, lemon zest and baking soda, combining well.

3. Pour the liquid mixture into the dry mixture, stirring to incorporate.

4. Using your hands, form the dough into Ping-Pong ball–size balls and place them on the prepared sheet pan. Using the bottom of a glass, the bottom of a jar or some other flat surface, flatten the dough balls so that they are about ¼ inch thick.

5. Bake the cookies for 10 to 15 minutes, or until they start to brown around the edges.

5 **Active hands-on time**

20 **Total time**

MOLASSES GINGER COOKIES

Yield: approximately 1 dozen cookies

I can't quite remember the name of the brand of ginger cookies we grew up with, but I do recall loving the flavor of those cookies, especially dunked in a glass of milk. To me, those cookies are a pure childhood comfort food. These cookies aren't exactly the same and they may not come from a box, but they are still reminiscent of my childhood and I hope you find them as comforting as I do! — *JULIE*

Parchment paper, for lining the sheet pan or cookie sheet

¼ cup organic unsulfered molasses

5 dates, pitted and pureed with 2 tablespoons water

3 large eggs

2 tablespoons coconut oil or ghee, melted

1 teaspoon vanilla extract

⅔ cup coconut flour

2 teaspoons ground ginger

1 teaspoon ground cinnamon

1 teaspoon baking soda

½ teaspoon sea salt

¼ teaspoon ground cloves

NOTE: If you don't have coconut flour, you can use almond flour instead. Just decrease the number of eggs to one and use 1½ cups of almond flour in place of the coconut flour.

1. Preheat the oven to 350°F. Line a sheet pan or cookie sheet with parchment paper.

2. With a hand mixer, in a food processor or by hand, combine the molasses, date paste, eggs, coconut oil or ghee, and vanilla in a medium-size mixing bowl.

3. In a small mixing bowl, combine the coconut flour, ginger, cinnamon, baking soda, salt and cloves.

4. Add the dry ingredients to the wet ingredients, and mix until well incorporated.

5. Using your hands or a tablespoon, form the dough into balls about the size of a golf ball. Place the dough balls on the sheet pan and flatten them with the bottom of a glass or another flat surface (grease the bottom of the glass with coconut oil to prevent sticking) so that they are about ¼ inch thick.

6. Bake the cookies for 9 to 11 minutes, or until they puff up slightly browned. Enjoy!

5-7 **Active hands-on time**

20 **Total time**

VARIATION: Adding a teaspoon or two of freshly grated ginger would bring a welcome kick to these cookies!

NOT NUTELLA

Yield: approximately 2 cups

We are not certain if there's been any other recipe we've posted on our blog that's gotten as much traffic as this one. Something about chocolate and hazelnuts seems to really appeal to people—and we can't blame them! This is a wildly simple sweet treat to prepare. When people ask us, "But what do you serve with this?" we usually answer, "Fresh berries, bananas or coconut," but in reality at our house a spoon is pretty much all we need.

2 cups hazelnuts, skins removed (blanched)

12 ounces good-quality dark chocolate (not unsweetened), broken into pieces

2 tablespoons coconut butter

NOTES: If you give this chocolate-hazelnut spread a thinner consistency, it makes for a nice dip for fruit (somewhat like fondue). To achieve this, add more chocolate and serve the spread while it is still warm, process the hazelnuts until they are really runny, or add a tablespoon of melted coconut oil.

1. Preheat the oven to 400°F. Place the hazelnuts on a large sheet pan and roast them for about 10 minutes, or until slightly browned. Be careful not to burn them.

2. Pour the hazelnuts into a food processor, and process until you've created hazelnut butter, about 5 to 7 minutes.

3. Place the chocolate pieces in a microwave-safe glass bowl, and microwave on high for 30 seconds. (Alternatively, you can melt the chocolate in a double boiler.) Stir well after 30 seconds and let the chocolate sit for a moment (the heat retained by the glass will help start the melting process). Microwave for another 30 seconds, and stir well. If the chocolate is not fully melted, microwave for another 30 seconds, repeating the process until the chocolate is fully melted.

4. Once the chocolate is fully melted, add the coconut butter and microwave for another 15 to 20 seconds.

5. Pour the melted chocolate-coconut mixture into the hazelnut butter, and process in the food processor until well blended.

6. Pour the chocolate-hazelnut spread into a small glass bowl. You can refrigerate it or serve it warm and still rather liquidy, or simply allow it to cool to room temperature, at which point it will have thickened and hardened somewhat.

15 **Active hands-on time**

15 **Total time**

NOTE that water and melted chocolate do not mix (water will cause your chocolate to seize). Make sure your bowl, the food processor and all the utensils used to stir the chocolate are completely dry!

PLANTAINS WITH COCONUT

Yield: 4-6 servings

Plantains are another one of those tropical foods that we wish grew in our back-yard. Plantains are versatile. You can go the savory *tostones* route by making some tasty chips (just don't use extremely ripe and sweet plantains for this), or, as in this recipe, use incredibly ripe, supersweet plantains and make a sweet treat. If you're feeling particularly indulgent, drizzle a little honey over these right before serving.

1 large egg

½ cup shredded coconut

2 large very ripe plantains, peeled and cut diagonally into ¾-inch slices

2 tablespoons coconut oil

NOTE: Make sure your plantains are incredibly ripe. You want the peels to be almost black—that's how you know the plantains will be plenty sweet.

1. Place the egg in a small bowl and the coconut in a separate small bowl. Beat the egg and dip each of the plantain slices into the egg, then into the coconut. Place them on a large plate until ready to sauté.

2. In a large skillet, heat the coconut oil over medium-high heat. The oil is ready when it sizzles if you put a drop of water in the skillet.

3. Once the oil is hot, carefully add the plantains, working in batches (depending on the size of your skillet), so the skillet is not overcrowded. Sauté for 3 to 5 minutes on each side, or until the coconut flakes are nice and brown, being careful not to burn.

4. Remove the plantains to a plate lined with paper towels and serve hot.

5-7 **Active hands-on time**

10 **Total time**

CONVERTING TO METRICS

Volume Measurement Conversions

U.S.	METRIC
¼ teaspoon	1.25 ml
½ teaspoon	2.5 ml
¾ teaspoon	3.75 ml
1 teaspoon	5 ml
1 tablespoon	15 ml
¼ cup	62.5 ml
½ cup	125 ml
¾ cup	187.5 ml
1 cup	250 ml

Weight Measurement Conversions

U.S.	METRIC
1 ounce	28.4 g
8 ounces	227.5 g
16 ounces (1 pound)	455 g

Cooking Temperature Conversions

Celsius/Centigrade: 0°C and 100°C are arbitrarily placed at the melting and boiling points of water and standard to the metric system.

Fahrenheit: Fahrenheit established 0°F as the stabilized temperature when equal amounts of ice, water and salt are mixed.

To convert temperatures in Fahrenheit to Celsius, use this formula: **C= (F-32) x 0.5555**

So, for example, if you are baking at 350°F and want to know that temperature in Celsius, use this calculation:
C = (350-32) x 0.5555=176.65°C

ACKNOWLEDGMENTS

Once upon a time, we were asked by some dear friends to write a cookbook. Looking back now, it seems impossible to fathom the impact that moment has had on our lives together. Even more difficult is recounting all the people who have inspired and supported us up to this point in our lives. Who knew that evening with friends, food and fellowship would bring us to this place? Isaac Newton has been quoted as saying, "If I have seen further, it is by standing on the shoulders of giants." Here is a brief tribute to some of those giants who have allowed us to see further than we could have ever seen ourselves.

Robb, Nicki and Zoe, *Paleo Comfort Foods* and *Quick & Easy Paleo Comfort Foods* exist because of you all and that fateful weekend in Jacksonville. Who would have guessed how much would have come out of that "cert"? We consider you part of our family and love you dearly. Thank you for your continued support and all you bring to our lives. Here's to many more laughs together, along with conch salad and cracked coconuts.

Jeff, Melissa and Gemma, it has been an amazing ride thus far and we look forward to many more years of playtime with the kids, dogs and us. We have you all to thank for our love of fitness, community and tasty vittles. Thank you for inspiring us and being a part of our journey.

Chrissy, Shawn, Kayden and Rylee, you're a part of that extended family, too, and it's because of you that we have no doubt that we'll be able to raise our son Paleo(ish), just like Kayden and Rylee. Thank you for inspiring us.

Mark Adams, our cookbooks would not be possible without your talented eye and creativity with the lens. You have brought the world into our kitchen twice now with your uncompromising attention to detail and your willingness to put your mouth where our food is. Thanks for the incredible photos and for volunteering to

sample every dish that has graced the pages of the *Paleo Comfort Foods* family of books. And to Lacey Holsenbeck, thank you for the countless hours of working with pesky crackers and troublesome sauces to make it all look right!

Our Local Three and Muss & Turner's family of amazing artists, how could we have done this without your help? Todd, Ryan and Chris, you have all stirred our imagination and demonstrated a passion for good food that is unequaled in Atlanta. Our palates and kitchen will never be the same thanks to your input and openness. We wish you continued success in health, fitness and inspiring the food patrons of our fair city.

A huge thanks to Sally Ekus and The Lisa Ekus Group for seeing talent in our passion and for believing in us. We have been overwhelmed by your support and guidance throughout this journey. Let's hope that we can keep you busy for many years to come.

Sarah and the rest of the team at Harlequin, we are so blessed to have your support and energy behind this book. What a journey this has been. Thank you for your patience and understanding during a most inspiring and challenging time in our lives. Your actions have shown us how much you care and trust our work.

We owe much of our success to the amazing Paleo and fitness communities, with which we're so grateful to be involved. Special thanks go to John and Kate Welbourn, Mat Lalonde, Sarah Johnson, Melissa Joulwan, Kyle Maynard, Michelle Tam and Henry Fong, Amy Kubal, Dallas and Melissa Hartwig, Patty and Ron Strilaeff and so many others: you all add so much to this community and inspire us to want to do more. Thank you for that. To the many readers, bloggers and supporters of the Paleo community and movement, there simply are no words to describe how much we love and appreciate you. Without your support, feedback and commitment to eating real food, this book would simply not be possible. There is still much work to be done. Showing the world that real food can be delicious, nourishing and fun is going to take a continued team effort. We promise to continue to do our best to bring tasty creations to your kitchen, and we hope that you all continue to share your incredible stories with anyone and everyone who will listen.

To our family, especially our parents, thank you for the love, support and willingness to listen when we needed an ear. To all the siblings, cousins, nieces and nephews who tried our recipes and put up with our constant advice on better eating, your enthusiasm has been a big help and motivator. Dylan, thanks for asking the tough questions and setting the example for making good choices when ordering food. You all have shaped us into the people we are today and we are forever grateful.

To our newborn son, Scott, we love you so very much. You inspire us to eat well, live well and make the world a better place. Your arrival in the midst of working on this book gave us a perspective we could have never known before now. Just so you know, you are a Paleo baby... so you're welcome! We look forward to many more years of sharing the joy of cooking with you.

INDEX

A

Aioli
Basil, 204
Lemon-Caper, 204
variations, 205

Almond butter, 5

Almond flour
Berry Scones, 226
Blueberry Muffins, 228
buying, 5
Herb Crackers, 30
Lemony Cookies, 234

Almond meal
Banana Muffins, 224
Salisbury Steak, 106

Almond(s)
buying, 5
-Crusted Pork Tenderloin, 80
Ginger-Garlic-Scallion Crusted Chicken, 136–37

Ancestral Health Society, 9

AncestryFoundation.org, 9

Anchovies
Bagna Càuda, 190

Apple(s)
buying, 4
-Cucumber Relish, 184
and Pear Sauce, 186
Sausage and, Dressing, 212

Apricot(s)
buying, 4
Lemony Cookies, 234

Artichokes
buying, 4
sauce for, 202

Arugula
Grilled Calamari Salad, 64
Pancetta Salad, 42

Sautéed Steaks with Tomato Pan Sauce and Wilted, 152

Asparagus
buying, 4
Sesame, 178
Szechuan Stir-Fry, 162

Avocado(s)
buying, 4, 5
Dipping Sauce, 166
oil, 5
Shrimp Cobb Salad, 48

B

Bacon
Arugula Pancetta Salad, 42
Basil-, Tomato Bites, 36
- and Basil-Wrapped Shrimp, 24
Clam Chowder, 46
Clams Casino, 26
Eggs Benedict Florentine, 125–26
Jam, 16
and Okra Pilau, 188
Pine Street Market's Meat of the Month Club for, 16
Sautéed Brussels Sprouts, 214
Shrimp Cobb Salad, 48

Bagna Càuda, 190

Baked Eggs with Vegetables, 122

BalancedBites.com, 9

Banana(s)
buying, 4
Muffins, 224

Barbecue Sauce, 168

Basil
Aioli, 204
Bacon- and, Wrapped Shrimp, 24
-Bacon Tomato Bites, 36
Pesto, 192

Quick Pesto Mayo, 154
Summer Squash Sauté, 220

BBTs (Basil-Bacon Tomato Bites), 36

Béarnaise Sauce, 203

Beef
Brunswick-ish Stew, 44
Kebabs, 82
Marinade, 82
Meat Loaf Muffins, 94
Pan-Sautéed Steaks with Creamy Leeks
    and Mushrooms, 142
Quick, Curry, 102
Salisbury Steak, 106–7
Sautéed Steaks with Tomato Pan Sauce
    and Wilted Arugula, 152
Speedy Gonzales Chili, 50
Steak Bites with Creamy Mushroom
    Sauce, 158
Steak Skewers, 22
Szechuan Stir-Fry, 162
Vegetable Meatza, 118

Beet(s)
buying, 4
Chutney, 80
Root Veggie Cakes, 210

Berry Scones, 226
variations, 227

Blackberry(ies)
Berry Scones, 226
buying, 4

Blueberry(ies)
Berry Scones, 226
buying, 4
frozen vs. fresh, 228
Muffins, 228

Bok choy, 4

Brazil nuts, 5

Broccoli
buying, 4
Chicken and, Casserole, 127–28
Quick Beef Curry, 102

Brown, Alton, 92

Brussels sprouts
buying, 4
Sautéed, 214

Burgers
Lamb, 90
sauce for (Tzatziki), 182
Thanksgiving, 116

Butter, 5

ghee (clarified butter), 5

Butternut squash
buying, 4
Green Turkey Chili, 62
Puree, 170
Roasted, Dip, 32

C

Cabbage
buying, 4
Garlicky Buttered, Noodles, 198

Calamari
Cioppino, 52
Salad, Grilled, 64

Cantaloupe
buying, 4
Chilled Melon Soup, 54

Caper(s)
Lemon-, Aioli, 204

**Carbohydrates, 3. See also fruits;
    vegetables**

Carrot(s)
buying, 4
Ginger-Glazed, 200
Root Veggie Cakes, 210

Cashews
Cilantro Pesto, 88
Date Balls, 230

Casseroles
Chicken and Broccoli, 127–28

Cauliflower
adding parsnips to, 208
buying, 4
Chicken and Broccoli Casserole, 127–28
Clam Chowder, 46
Creamy, and Chicken Soup, 56
Sweet and Savory Roasted, 180

Cauliflower Rice
Bacon and Okra Pilau, 188
Brunswick-ish Stew, 44

Lime and Coconut Chicken "Rice," 140
Paella, 77–78
Quick Beef Curry, 102
recipe for, 45

Celeriac, 4

Celery
buying, 4
Sausage and Apple Dressing, 212

Cherry(ies)
buying, 4
Chutney, 80

Chicken
Bacon- and Basil-Wrapped Shrimp
(variation), 24
and Broccoli Casserole, 127–28
Brunswick-ish Stew, 44
Creamy Cauliflower and, Soup, 56
Creamy Shrimp Fra Diavolo (variation),
135
Eleanor's Wings, 28–29
Fried, Tenders, 86
Ginger-Garlic-Scallion Crusted, 136–37
Lime and Coconut, "Rice," 140
with Mustard Sauce, 132
Quick Beef Curry (variation), 102
Quick Coq au Vin, 146
Quick Roasted Whole, 148
Red Curry, 150
Saltimbocca, 130
Southwestern Shepherd's Pie, 113–14
Tortilla-Less Soup, 70

Chili
Green Turkey, 62
Speedy Gonzales, 50
Chilies (green). See also Chipotle
peppers or powder; Jalapeño(s);
Poblano chilies
Spicy Plum Sauce, 218

Chilled Melon Soup, 54

Chipotle peppers or powder
Green Turkey Chili, 62
Mashed Sweet Potatoes, 194
Rosemary Nuts, 34
Southwestern Shepherd's Pie, 113
Sweet Potato, Spinach and Chorizo
Stew, 68

Chocolate
Not Nutella, 238

tip on heating, 239

Chorizo
Paella, 77–78
Sweet Potato, Spinach and, Stew, 68

ChrisKresser.com, 9

Chutney, 80

Cilantro
Peach Salsa, 206
Pesto, 88
Tortilla-Less Soup, 70

Cioppino, 52

Clam(s)
Casino, 26
Chowder, 46
Paella, 77–78

Coconut
buying, 5
Date Balls, 230
Island Balls, 232
Nutless Balls, 231
Plantains with, 240

Coconut butter
Not Nutella, 238

Coconut flour
Molasses Ginger Cookies, 236

Coconut milk
buying, 5
Clam Chowder, 46
Creamy Cauliflower and Chicken Soup,
56
Creamy Tomato Soup, 58

Coconut oil, 5

Collards
buying, 4
Sautéed Kale with a Kick (variation), 217

Conversion table, 242

Cookies
Lemony, 234
Molasses Ginger, 236

Coq au Vin, Quick, 146

Cordain, Loren, 8

Crab
Stuffed Flounder, 110–12

Crackers, Herb, 30

Cranberry(ies)
Chutney, 80

Creamy Cauliflower and Chicken Soup, 56

Creamy Shrimp Fra Diavolo, 134

Creamy Tomato Soup, 58

Cucumber(s)
Apple-, Relish, 184
buying, 4
Greek Salad, 60
Tzatziki Sauce, 182

Curry/Curried
Deviled Eggs, 18
Noodles, 196
Quick Beef, 102
Red, Chicken, 150

D

Daikon, 4

Date(s)
Balls, 230
Island Balls, 232
Molasses Ginger Cookies, 236
Nutless Balls, 231
Sweet and Savory Roasted Cauliflower, 180

Dips
accompaniments for, 30
Apple-Cucumber Relish, 184
Avocado Dipping Sauce, 166
Bagna Càuda, 190
Basil Aioli, 204
Lemon-Caper Aioli, 204
Not Nutella, 238
Quick Pesto Mayo, 192
Roasted Butternut Squash, 32

Dirty Dozen and Clean 15, 4

Dressing, Sausage and Apple, 212

Druid Hills Golf Club, 136

E

Eggplant
buying, 4
Quick Beef Curry, 102

Egg(s)
Baked, with Vegetables, 122
Benedict Florentine, 125–26
Blueberry Muffins, 228
buying, 3
Curried Deviled, 18
hard-boiling, 18
Hollandaise Sauce, 202
Molasses Ginger Cookies, 236
Old-Fashioned Fiesta Omelets, 96–97
Paleo Mayonnaise, 204
poaching, 126
as protein, 3
Quick Skillet Frittata, 104
Salad, 84
Shrimp Cobb Salad, 48

Eleanor's bar, 28

Eleanor's Wings, 28–29

Environmental Working Group (EWG)'s Dirty Dozen and Clean 15, 4

F

Fats, 5
adding to skillet, 101
sources recommended, 5

Fennel, 4

Fig(s)
buying, 4
Lamb Chops with, and Olives, 138

Fish. See also Seafood
as protein, 3
buying, 3
Cioppino, 52
Halibut with Cilantro Pesto, 88
Macadamia Nut-Crusted Mahimahi, 92
Paella, 77–78
Pan-Seared Sole, 98
Seared Salmon with Quick Pesto Mayo, 154
Spicy Salmon Cakes, 156
Stuffed Flounder, 110–12

Flounder, 88, 98
buying tip, 110
Stuffed, 110–12

Food, Inc. (film), 6
Fried Chicken Tenders, 86
Fruits
  buying tip, 3
  Dirty Dozen and Clean 15, 4

G

Garlic
  Bagna Càuda, 190
  buying, 4
  Garlicky Buttered Cabbage Noodles, 198
  Ginger-, Scallion Crusted Chicken, 136–37
Ghee (clarified butter), 5
Ginger
  -Garlic-Scallion Crusted Chicken, 136–37
  -Glazed Carrots, 200
  Molasses, Cookies, 236
Grapefruit
  buying, 4
  Jicama, Pear and, Salad, 66
Grape(s), 4
Greek Salad, 60
Green Turkey Chili, 62
Gum Creek Farms, 160

H

Halibut with Cilantro Pesto, 88
Hall, Chris, 54, 214
Ham
  Old-Fashioned Fiesta Omelets, 96–97
  Shrimp Cobb Salad, 48
Hartwig, Dallas and Melissa, 6, 8
Hazelnuts
  buying, 5
  Not Nutella, 238
Herb(s)
  Crackers, 30
  growing, 7
Hollandaise Sauce, 202
  Eggs Benedict Florentine, 125–26

Holy Taco restaurant, 180
Homemade "Lärabar" Balls, Three Ways, 230–32
Horseradish
  buying, 210
  Root Veggie Cakes, 210

J

Jalapeño(s)
  Green Turkey Chili, 62
  handling tip, 20
  Peach Salsa, 206
  Poppers, 20
  Sautéed Kale with a Kick, 216
  Tortilla-Less Soup, 70
Jam
  Bacon, 16
Jicama
  Apple-Cucumber Relish, 184
  buying, 4
  Pear and Grapefruit Salad, 66
  Seasoned, Fries, 176

K

Kale
  buying, 4
  Sautéed, with a Kick, 216
Kiwi, 4
Kohlrabi, 4

L

Lamb
  Burgers, 90
  Chops with Figs and Olives, 138
  Tzatziki Sauce for, 182
Lard, 5
Leeks
  Pan-Sautéed Steaks with Creamy, and Mushrooms, 142
Leidenfrost effect, 101
Lemon(s)
  buying, 4
  -Caper Aioli, 204

Lemony Cookies, 234

Lettuce. See also Romaine Lettuce
buying, 4

Lime(s)
buying, 4
and Coconut Chicken "Rice," 140
juice, tip for using, 207

Local Three restaurant, 28, 38, 54, 214
"Paleo night," 38, 54

M

Macadamia nut(s), 5
-Crusted Mahimahi, 92
Island Balls, 232

Mahimahi
Macadamia Nut-Crusted, 92

Mango(es)
buying, 4
Tropical Salsa, 144

Marinade
for beef, 82

MarksDailyApple.com, 8

Mayonnaise, Paleo, 204
Quick Pesto Mayo, 154

Meat (red) and game
cooking, 101
as protein, 3
Spicy Plum Sauce for, 218

Meat Loaf Muffins, 94

Melvin, Nick, 20

Mint
Peach Salsa, 206

Molasses Ginger Cookies, 236

Muffins
Banana, 224
Blueberry, 228
Meat Loaf, 94

Mushroom(s)
Baked Eggs with Vegetables, 122
buying, 4
Creamy, Sauce, 158
Old-Fashioned Fiesta Omelets, 96–97
Pan-Sautéed Steaks with Creamy Leeks
and, 142

Quick Coq au Vin, 146
Salisbury Steak, 106–7
Sausage and Apple Dressing, 212
Sautéed, 174
Seared Scallops with Onion-, Sauce, 108
Stuffed Pork Chops, 160
Vegetable Meatza, 118

Muss & Turner's restaurant, 28, 32

Mussman, Todd, 20, 28, 174

Mustard Sauce, 132

N

Nectarine(s), 4

Nishiyama, Jonn "Nish," 136

Not Nutella, 238

Nutless Balls, 231

Nuts
Date Balls, 230
Island Balls, 232
Not Nutella, 238
phytic acid in, 231
Rosemary, 34

O

Oatmeal, The (blog), 156

Okra
Bacon and, Pilau, 188
buying, 4
Pan-Fried, 172

Old-Fashioned Fiesta Omelets, 96–97

Olive oil, 5

Olive(s), 5
Egg Salad, 84
Greek Salad, 60
Lamb Chops with Figs and, 138
Sweet and Savory Roasted Cauliflower,
180
Tuna, Salad, 72
Vegetable Meatza, 118

Onion(s)
Baked Eggs with Vegetables, 122
Beef Kebabs, 82
buying, 4
Clams Casino, 26

Greek Salad, 60
Old-Fashioned Fiesta Omelets, 96–97
Peach Salsa, 206
Quick Beef Curry, 102
Quick Coq au Vin, 146
Sausage and Apple Dressing, 212
Sautéed Kale with a Kick, 216
Seared Scallops with, -Mushroom
    Sauce, 108
Smothered Pork Chops, 120
Spicy Plum Sauce, 218
Summer Squash Sauté, 220
Vegetable Meatza, 118

Organic foods
    buying fruits and vegetables, 3
    eggs, 3
    fish and seafood, 3
    meats and poultry, 3

P

Paella, 77–78

Paleo foods, 3–5
    as anti-inflammatory, 5
    bottled sauces, 22
    buying local agriculture, 6
    carbohydrates, 3
    fats, 5
    herbs (fresh), 7
    individualizing, food matrix, 5
    "Meat on a stick," 82
    pantry staples, 10
    planting a garden, 6, 7
    protein, 3, 103
    substitution for noodles, 196
    what isn't included, 5

Paleo lifestyle, 6
    books for, 9
    helpful tips and tricks, 12–13
    pantry staples, 10
    repositioning mind and palate, 176
    tools and equipment basics, 10

Paleo Mayonnaise, 204
    Quick Pesto Mayo, 154
    substitutions for, 19

Paleo resources
    AncestryFoundation.org, 9
    BalancedBites.com, 9

ChrisKresser.com, 9
MarksDailyApple.com, 8
RobbWolf.com, 8
ThePaleoDiet.com, 8
Whole9Life.com, 8

Paleo Solution, The (Wolf), 8

Pancetta
    Arugula, Salad, 42

Pan-Fried Okra, 172

Pan-Sautéed Steaks with Creamy Leeks
    and Mushrooms, 142

Pantry staples, 10

Parsnip(s)
    Roasted Mashed, 208
    Root Veggie Cakes, 210

Peach(es)
    buying, 4
    Salsa, 206

Pear(s)
    Apple and, Sauce, 186
    buying, 4
    Jicama, and Grapefruit Salad, 66

Pecan(s), 5
    Arugula Pancetta Salad, 42
    Banana Muffins, 224

Peppercorns, Szechuan, 162

Peppers (bell)
    Beef Kebabs, 82
    buying, 4
    Clams Casino, 26
    Curry Noodles, 196
    Pork Medallions and, 100
    Quick Beef Curry, 102
    Sesame Asparagus, 178
    Southwestern Shepherd's Pie, 113–14
    Speedy Gonzales Chili, 50
    Szechuan Stir-Fry, 162
    Vegetable Meatza, 118

Pesto
    Basil, 192
    Cilantro, 88
    Quick, Mayo, 154

Pilau, Bacon and Okra, 188

Pineapple(s), 4

Pine nuts
    Basil Pesto, 192

Pine Street Market, 16, 42, 160
Meat of the Month Club, 16

Plantains
with Coconut, 240
tostones, 240

Plum(s)
Spicy, Sauce, 218

Poblano chilies
Green Turkey Chili, 62
Tortilla-Less Soup, 70

Pork
Almond-Crusted, Tenderloin, 80
Brunswick-ish Stew, 44
Chops with Tropical Salsa, 144
Medallions and Peppers, 100
as protein, 3
quick pan sauce for chops, 161
Sausage and Apple Dressing, 212
Smothered, Chops, 120
source for, 160
Stuffed, Chops, 160

Pork rinds
Fried Chicken Tenders, 86
Macadamia Nut-Crusted Mahimahi, 92
replacing panko crumbs, 92

Poultry. See also Chicken; Turkey
as protein, 3
seasoning, 213

Practical Paleo (Sanfilippo), 9

Prosciutto
Chicken Saltimbocca, 130

Protein
eggs, 3
fish and seafood, 3
pork, 3
poultry, 3
quick cooking types, 103
red meat and game, 3

Pumpkin
buying, 4
Roasted Butternut Squash Dip
(variation), 33

Quick Beef Curry, 102
Quick Coq au Vin, 146
Quick Skillet Frittata, 104
Quick Roasted Whole Chicken, 148

R

Radishes, 4

Raisins
Almond-Crusted Pork Tenderloin, 80
Berry Scones (variation), 226
Chutney, 80
Lemony Cookies, 234

Raspberry(ies)
Berry Scones, 226
buying, 4

Relish
Apple-Cucumber, 184

Rhubarb, 4

Rice. See Cauliflower

Roasted Butternut Squash Dip, 32

Roasted Mashed Parsnips, 208

RobbWolf.com, 8

Romaine lettuce
Greek Salad, 60
Shrimp Cobb Salad, 48

Root Veggie Cakes, 210
variations, 211

Rosemary
growing, 7
Nuts, 34
Sautéed Brussels Sprouts, 214
Sweet and Savory Roasted Cauliflower,
180

S

Sage
Chicken Saltimbocca, 130
poultry seasoning, 213
Sausage and Apple Dressing, 212
Sautéed Mushrooms, 174
Stuffed Pork Chops, 160

Salad dressings
　　Basil Aioli, 204
　　for Greek Salad, 60
　　Lemon-Caper Aioli, 204
　　Paleo Mayonnaise, 204

Salads
　　Arugula Pancetta, 42
　　Egg, 84
　　Greek, 60
　　Grilled Calamari, 64
　　Jicama, Pear and Grapefruit, 66
　　Shrimp Cobb, 48
　　Tuna Olive, 72

Salisbury Steak, 106–7

Salmon
　　canned wild-caught, 157
　　fresh wild-caught, when to buy, 154
　　Seared, with Quick Pesto Mayo, 154
　　Spicy, Cakes, 156

Salsa
　　Peach, 206
　　Tropical, 144

Saltimbocca, Chicken, 130

Sanfilippo, Diane, 9

Sauces
　　Apple and Pear, 186
　　Avocado Dipping, 166
　　Bagna Càuda, 190
　　Barbecue, 168
　　Basil Aioli, 204
　　béarnaise, 203
　　Creamy Mushroom, 158
　　Hollandaise, 202
　　Lemon-Caper Aioli, 204
　　Mustard, 132
　　quick pan, for pork chops, 161
　　Spicy Plum, 218
　　Tomato Pan, 152
　　Tzatziki, 182

Sausage
　　and Apple Dressing, 212
　　Paella, 77–78
　　Quick Skillet Frittata, 104
　　Sweet Potato, Spinach and Chorizo
　　　　Stew, 68
　　Thanksgiving Burgers, 116

Sautéed Brussels Sprouts, 214

Sautéed Kale with a Kick, 216

Sautéed Mushrooms, 174

Sautéed Steaks with Tomato Pan Sauce
　　and Wilted Arugula, 152

Scallion(s)
　　Ginger-Garlic-, Crusted Chicken,
　　　　136–37
　　Root Veggie Cakes, 210

Scallop(s)
　　Bacon- and Basil-Wrapped Shrimp
　　　　(variation), 24
　　Cioppino, 52
　　cooking tip, 108
　　Creamy Shrimp Fra Diavolo (variation),
　　　　135
　　Grilled Calamari Salad (variation), 65
　　Quick Beef Curry (variation), 103
　　Seared, with Onion-Mushroom Sauce,
　　　　108

Seafood
　　Cioppino, 52
　　Clam Chowder, 46
　　Creamy Shrimp Fra Diavolo, 134
　　Grilled Calamari Salad, 64
　　Paella, 77–78
　　Seared Scallops with Onion-Mushroom
　　　　Sauce, 108
　　Shrimp Cobb Salad, 48

Searcy, Tommy, 20

Seared Salmon with Quick Pesto Mayo,
　　154

Seared Scallops with Onion-Mushroom
　　Sauce, 108

Seasoned Jicama Fries, 176

Sesame
　　Asparagus, 178
　　oil, using, 178

Shrimp
　　Bacon- and Basil-Wrapped, 24
　　Cobb Salad, 48
　　Creamy, Fra Diavolo, 134
　　Grilled Calamari Salad (variation), 65
　　Jalapeño Poppers, 20
　　Paella, 77–78
　　Quick Beef Curry (variation), 103

Sisson, Mark, 8
Skewers (meat on a stick)
  Beef Kebabs, 82
  Steak, 22
Smothered Pork Chops, 120
Sole, 88
  buying tip, 98
  Pan-Seared, 98
Soups
  Chilled Melon, 54
  Cioppino, 52
  Clam Chowder, 46
  Creamy Cauliflower and Chicken, 56
  Creamy Tomato, 58
  Tortilla-Less, 70
Southwestern Shepherd's Pie, 113–14
Speedy Gonzales Chili, 50
Spice blend, 28–29
Spicy Salmon Cakes, 156
Spinach
  Baked Eggs with Vegetables, 122
  buying, 4
  Eggs Benedict Florentine, 125–26
  Sweet Potato, and Chorizo Stew, 68
Squash, summer
  buying, 4
  Curry Noodles, 196
  Sauté, 220
Squash, winter
  Butternut Squash Puree, 170
  buying, 4
  Green Turkey Chili, 62
  Roasted Butternut Squash Dip, 32
Sriracha, 156
  Spicy Salmon Cakes, 156
Steak Skewers, 22
Stews
  Brunswick-ish, 44
  Sweet Potato, Spinach and Chorizo, 68
Strawberry(ies)
  Berry Scones, 226
  buying, 4

Stuffed Flounder, 110–12
Stuffed Pork Chops, 160
Sunflower seed butter, 5
Sunflower seed(s), 5
  Nutless Balls, 231
Sur La Table restaurant, 34
Sweet and Savory Roasted Cauliflower, 180
Sweet potato(es)
  buying, 4
  Chipotle Mashed, 194
  Quick Skillet Frittata, 104
  Southwestern Shepherd's Pie, 113–14
  Spinach and Chorizo Stew, 68
Swift, Jay, 20
Szechuan Stir-Fry, 162
  peppercorns for, 162

T

Taco or fajita seasoning, 71
Tahini, 5
Tallow, 5
Thai chili peppers
  Quick Beef Curry, 102
Thanksgiving Burgers, 116
ThePaleoDiet.com, 8
Tips and tricks, 12–13
Tomatillos
  Green Turkey Chili, 62
Tomato(es)
  Arugula Pancetta Salad, 42
  Bacon Jam, 16
  Baked Eggs with Vegetables, 122
  Barbecue Sauce, 168
  Basil-Bacon, Bites, 36
  Brunswick-ish Stew, 44
  buying, 4
  Cioppino, 52
  Creamy Shrimp Fra Diavolo, 134
  Creamy, Soup, 58
  cutting tip, 38
  Greek Salad, 60
  Grilled Calamari Salad, 64
  Paella, 77–78

Pan Sauce, 152
Peach Salsa, 206
Shrimp Cobb Salad, 48
Southwestern Shepherd's Pie, 113–14
Speedy Gonzales Chili, 50
Summer Squash Sauté, 220
Tartare, 38
Tortilla-Less Soup, 70
Vegetable Meatza, 118

Tools and equipment basics, 10

Tortilla-Less Soup, 70

Tropical Salsa, 144

Tuna, 3
Olive Salad, 72

Turkey
Green, Chili, 62
Southwestern Shepherd's Pie, 113–14
Thanksgiving Burgers, 116

Tzatziki Sauce, 182

U

Union Square Cafe, 34

V

Vegetable(s)
Baked Eggs with, 122
buying tip, 3
Dirty Dozen and Clean 15, 4
Meatza, 118
Root Veggie Cakes, 210

Violetti, Nicki, 52

W

Walnut(s), 5
Basil Pesto, 192
Date Balls, 230

Watermelon, 4

Whole9Life.com, 8

Whole30, 8

Wine, red
Creamy Mushroom Sauce, 158
Quick Coq au Vin, 146

Wolf, Robb, 52

Y

Yes Ma'am band, 180

Z

Zucchini
Curry Noodles, 196
Summer Squash Sauté, 220